D1029110

MONEY AND THE COMING
WORLD ORDER

LEHRMAN INSTITUTE BOOKS

The Lehrman Institute was founded in 1972 as a private, nonprofit, operating foundation devoted to the analysis of public policy in its broadest aspects, with particular emphasis on the historical roots of contemporary policy questions. The Institute encourages interdisciplinary study—so as to foster a greater awareness of the interpenetration of history, politics, and economics—and also contributes to nonpartisan debate on contemporary policy issues. To these ends, the Institute sponsors annually a program of seminars organized around the works-in-progress of a small number of appointed Research Fellows and also conducts other series of study groups, focusing on major problems in foreign affairs and economic policy. These seminars bring together scholars, businessmen, journalists, and public servants.

Beginning in early 1976, the Institute will arrange to publish certain books under its aegis which will include specially commissioned essays and other monographs which were originally presented as working papers in Institute seminars and which, in the judgment of the Trustees of the Institute, are worthy of presentation to a wider public.

The Lehrman Institute does not take any position with regard to any issue: all statements of fact and expression of opinion in these publications are the sole responsibility of the individual authors. The Institute is not affiliated with, nor does it receive funds from, any educational institution or any agency of the United States Government.

MONEY AND THE COMING WORLD ORDER

David P. Calleo, *Editor*
Harold van B. Cleveland
Charles P. Kindleberger
Lewis E. Lehrman

A Lehrman Institute Book
published by
New York University Press • 1976

CONTENTS

LIST OF CONTRIBUTORS

DAVID P. CALLEO received his undergraduate and graduate degrees at Yale, taught there, served as consultant to the U. S. Undersecretary of State for Political Affairs, and is now Professor of European Studies at The Johns Hopkins School of Advanced International Studies in Washington, and Vice-Chairman for Academic Affairs at the Lehrman Institute. He is the author, among other works, of *Europe's Future: The Grand Alternatives* (1965); *Coleridge and the Idea of the Modern State* (1966); *Britain's Future* (1968); *The Atlantic Fantasy: The U.S., N.A.T.O., and Europe* (1970); and (with Benjamin M. Rowland) *America and the World Political Economy* (1973).

HAROLD van B. CLEVELAND received his undergraduate and law degrees at Harvard, and subsequently served as Assistant Chief in the Division of Investment and Economic Development, Department of State; Deputy Director and Special Economic Advisor, European Program Division, Economic Cooperation Administration; International Economist and Assistant Director of Research, Committee for Economic Development; and Director of Atlantic Policy Studies at the Council on Foreign Relations. He is currently Vice President at the Economics Department of the First National City Bank, and a Trustee of the Lehrman Institute. He is co-author (with Theodore Geiger) of *The Political Economy of Ameri-*

can *Foreign Policy* (1955), and author of *The Atlantic Idea and its European Rivals* (1966).

CHARLES P. KINDLEBERGER did his graduate work at Columbia, and is currently Professor of Economics at M.I.T. During the war he served on the O. S. S.; and from 1945-48 he was Chief of the division of German and Austrian Economic Affairs in the Department of State. He is the author of numerous studies including: *International Short-Term Capital Movements* (1937); *The Dollar Shortage* (1950); *International Economics* (1953); *Economic Development* (1958); *Foreign Trade and the National Economy* (1962); *Economic Growth in France and Britain, 1851-1950* (1964); *American Business Abroad* (1969); *Power and Money* (1970); *The World in Depression, 1929-39* (1973).

LEWIS E. LEHRMAN is President of Rite Aid Corporation, and Chairman of the Board of Trustees of the Lehrman Institute. He received his undergraduate training at Yale, where he was subsequently a Carnegie Teaching Fellow in history, and a M.A. in history from Harvard (where he was a Woodrow Wilson Fellow). He is currently a member of the Yale University Council; chairman of the visiting Committee for the Study of the Humanities; and a trustee of the American Enterprise Institute.

INTRODUCTION

I

In recent years, international political economy, long the preserve of the Marxists, has come into general scholarly fashion. Widespread interest has developed in the interdependence of political and economic patterns. International economic policy, once regarded as a somewhat dreary specialty, is now considered not only of great importance, but also closely related to general political and military policy. None of this, needless to say, should come as a great revelation. The Marxists, of course, have always preached it. But the insight was scarcely their monopoly. American leaders, in laying the foundations of the postwar system, were keenly aware of the linkage. It was, for example, Franklin Delano Roosevelt's Secretary of the Treasury, Henry Morganthau, who described the UN Security Council and the International Monetary Fund as the two blades of a pair of scissors. No one who has struggled through Cordell Hull's memoirs, nor indeed who has read General de Gaulle's, can doubt the significance of economic issues in the postwar strategies of the great powers. In addition, a quick look at the interwar period, or into those fundamental conflicts which led to the First World War, equally confirms the intimacy of economic and political goals.

Ironically, only during the Cold War, presumably a duel between two rival political-economic world systems, did scholars focus so exclusively upon the military and generally noneconomic dimensions of international relations. But as the apocalyptic geopolitical visions of that theatrical era have receded and the nations of the world have returned to their more normal situations, the mutual autonomy of "high politics" and "low politics" has gradually come to an end, even among the scholarly specialists who study such matters.

An obvious reason for this renewed interest in economic questions is the evident malaise which has now settled upon the world economic order. A deep and stubborn recession, unprecedented unemployment, the simultaneous spectre of runaway inflation, plus a threatened breakdown of stable prices and supplies of raw materials all provide a new setting for international politics. Conflict among the Western powers, which used to revolve around such relatively harmless questions as the command structure of NATO, has now turned to exchange rates and commercial policies, all matters of great sensitivity for domestic politics. And these economic conflicts in the West are beginning to take on sharpness reminiscent of an era whose troubles we had thought behind us.

Many analysts see the present difficulties not merely as an unfortunate conjunction of specific national and international ailments, but as a more general disorder of the world system itself. For many, the key to this disorder lies in the gradual erosion of American hegemony over both the noncommunist industrial world and the "Third World." That hegemony built the present world system. It is a structure inspired not only by postwar anticommunism but also by a liberal federalist idealism—a creed nurtured as the American political imagination long anticipated the world leadership which history so obviously had ordained. The American global system has had many virtues. Under its influence, the world has enjoyed a time of prosperity and tranquillity unusual in the tumultuous modern era. But, American hegemony has seemingly grown weaker with the very success of the system which it has built. With the reconstruction of Europe and Japan, American political and economic predominance has inevitably diminished, and the continuing subordinate roles of the other major capitalist states have grown more anomalous. Moreover, the decolonization and "development" of the Third World has brought about a heightened and more effective dissatisfaction with the global status quo. All these predictable trends have become more evident since the later sixties and culminate, many believe, in the present systemic crisis. In this book, we take as our common point of departure the view that the postwar world political-economic system is radically transforming itself, if not breaking down.

II

A new consciousness of the interdependence of power and money gives economists and businessmen a new basis for conducting a mutually interesting discourse. And the interest extends not only to economists and businessmen, but also to those political scientists and historians concerned with power in political, military and diplomatic spheres.

The Lehrman Institute, as a small foundation devoted to the analysis of international policy questions, has tried to provide occasions for exploring these mutual concerns. The particular Lehrman study group which gave rise to this volume called itself "New Modes of Economic Order." Separate seminar sessions in the spring of 1975 discussed the four papers. Each was designed to offer a different insight into the question of the postwar world political economy and its probable evolution. All focused heavily on the monetary system

—not only because of its central importance, but because it serves as a sort of metaphor for the political-economic system in general.*

All four of the authors in addition to their practical involvements, share a strong historical and philosophical interest in political-economic issues. None of the authors, I expect, would regard his chapter as the last word on so vast and complicated a subject. All of the original papers were designed to provoke spirited discussions at the time and more tranquil reflection later. The participants in the seminar discussions were a similar group of businessmen, journalists, and academics from many disciplines. The meetings were generally thought to be a considerable success. Certainly the sessions were lively, the participants well-prepared, and the attendance impressive.

III

The four chapters represent a broad spectrum, even if other important views are not represented. The papers are rich and concise and summarizing cannot do them justice.

Each of the authors shares the belief that the hegemonial postwar system has been changing rapidly. All also accept the view that the monetary order in particular and the political-economic order in general tend to reflect the overall international distribution of power. Of the four, Harold van Buren Cleveland is the least alarmed by the contemporary picture. The present monetary system of managed floating, he believes, is a reasonably accurate expression of an untidy world system whose hegemon, while declining, is still very powerful. Cleveland suggests, moreover, that this untidy system is, in itself, a workable and stable order, likely to persist indefinitely. The others have a more pessimistic view. Charles Kindleberger, for reasons which he explains, believes a system is unlikely to function well without a leader. Since he has only tepid hope for any single or collective hegemon to replace a United States afflicted by entropy, his outlook is cautiously pessimistic.

Lewis Lehrman and I, if more apocalyptic, are also more optimistic. Unlike Cleveland, I believe the present tension between lingering hegemony and uncertain pluralism is unstable and will lead national states, disrupted internally by an increasingly chaotic world system, to withdraw into blocs. Ultimately, I hope, the blocs will consolidate and the political and cultural preconditions for a stable plural system will emerge. If not, I fear the present degeneration will lead to domestic and international catastrophe.

Lehrman is preoccupied with the problem of how money can again be made to perform its fundamental purpose—to mediate between infinite desires and lmited resources. A hegemonial or reserve-currency system leads inevitably, he believes, to inflation which cannot, for reasons he explains, be contained within one country. Ultimately, as Lehrman sees it, a system characterized by increasingly unmanageable levels of public and private debt must collapse—to be replaced, he hopes, by a liberal system of rapid convertibility. In his new system, international discipline will reinforce domestic discipline. Like the eighteenth century after the excesses of the seventeenth, the late twentieth century will move to a new era of restraint and reason.

Each of the four positions is, of course, open to serious attack. Cleveland adopts a view no doubt more likely than not to be correct in the short run. Nonetheless, his complacency over the evolution of economic events during the past decade is not altogether easy to accept. The present system clearly does, as he says, represent a sort of negotiated compromise; but whether that compromise is stable, or whether negotiations will not degenerate into increasingly sharp conflict, are questions about which others may have less sanguine views. Systems, after all, tend to collapse into wars and depressions in precisely such periods of contest and uncertainty.

Kindleberger's enthusiasm for hegemony is arguable on both historical and philosophical grounds. He is, of course, a most distinguished advocate of that historical view which attributes peaceful order and prosperity in the nineteenth century to Britain's hegemony. Germany's challenge and America's failure to assume Britain's place are the broad causes, in this view, of the great troubles of our century. Advocates of the balance of power will perhaps not accept such a reading of history, nor accept the philosophical premise behind it. "Power corrupts" remains an axiom not altogether disproved by imperial histories—even that of the United States. And, it can be argued that the foundation of peace in the nineteenth century was not Britain's overweening empire, but the balance of power established at Vienna. Among the things which destroyed that balance, it might be said, was the threat to the others constituted by the excessive growth of imperial Britain and the rise of powers on the scale of Russia and America.

But those who would reject Kindleberger's hegemonial theory of history must still answer his questions: From where else can come the "leadership" for the general good? How will the system of rules and habits be managed? Who will provide the market for distress goods, discount freely in crises, and, in general, look after the public good?

If Kindleberger's paper is baroque, with order imposed by power, Lehrman's is classical, with order springing from natural law. His is that rationalistic view of economics and human affairs typical of Jacques Rueff and, indeed, of the classical liberal tradition of the gold standard. Lehrman's abhorrence of political interference with market discipline will not, however, be shared by everyone. Even those who might admire it will wonder if it is a feasible regimen for today's mercantilist, welfare states. In fact, as I try to state in my own piece, the question of returning to a monetary system which encourages restraint becomes ever more urgent; the postwar panacea of endless growth and inflation seems ever more precarious. Lehrman's issue is increasingly difficult to dismiss.

If not his market discipline, then what is to restore equilibrium? Are modern democratic states capable of achieving, through politics, a successful general will, including an efficient and just distribution of income? It should be noted, in passing, that the lack of economic discipline which so disturbs Lehrman is hardly a peculiar weakness of the left, a point which he himself makes. It is not just welfare for the poor which unbalances national budgets, but also huge subsidies to unprofitable enterprise or the insatiable consumption of bloated bureaucratic and educational establishments. No one examining the present American budget, for example, can easily overlook the still unbridled expenditures on arms.

My article can doubless be criticized on numerous historical or philosophical grounds. Like Cleveland, and unlike Lehrman or Kindleberger, I am more or less a relativist on the question of the "best" structure of the international monetary order. But unlike Cleveland, I do not believe the present uneasy balance between decaying hegemony and reluctant pluralism can long remain economically stable or politically peaceful. Whether I am right to expect a European bloc to form, or to have the benign systemic effects which I anticipate, are obviously matters subject to great difference of opinion.

In any event, I hope that I have said enough to give an idea of what follows and to whet the reader's appetite. Whatever their virtues and failures, the four chapters together should open new perspectives to those who are trying to perceive the structure of a rapidly changing world. It is in this spirit that we present them.

David P. Calleo

* These seminars were made possible, in part, through a grant from the Charles E. Merrill Trust, which the Lehrman Institute gratefully acknowledges.

MODES OF INTERNATIONAL ECONOMIC ORGANIZATION: A STALEMATE SYSTEM

Harold van B. Cleveland

Some years ago, Stanley Hoffmann described the emerging system of international order as "a stalemate system of international relations." It was, he said, "a system in which all nations find it easier to deter than to advance—and not only in purely military terms." [1] I propose here that the international economic system that exists among the industrial countries, and between them and developing countries, can also be usefully thought of in this way. It is a system which has a certain structural stability and which is able to preserve a relatively open and expansive international economic environment, despite the failure—or partial failure—of the organizing principles that are usually thought to be necessary to maintain such an economic order: agreed rules of conduct, leadership by a hegemonic power, or a harmonious balance of power in the classical sense. The contemporary "stalemate system" has, to be sure, elements of all three of these principles. There are some accepted rules in the fields of trade and money, and an important element of central leadership in the military and monetary spheres.

1

The present system has a good deal in common, too, with a balance-of-power system of the kind exemplified by the Concert of Europe. For the principal actors are prevented by countervailing power from trying to alter or reform the system, structurally, in their own favor. But it differs from a balance-of-power system in the inequality of some of the principal actors, in the presence of relatively stable alignments (classical balance-of-power politics presupposes frequent shifts of alignment), and in the high level of frustration and tension that underlies the structural stability. In the classical balance-of-power system, the moderation of means was matched by the moderation of ends. In the contemporary stalemate system, the ends of the principal actors have frequently been immoderate. Witness the grandiose pretensions of Kennedy's and Johnson's (and even Nixon's) America, not to mention Kruscheff's or even Brezhneff's Russia and de Gaulle's France. But the realization of immoderate ends—ends which imply major changes in the system—is effectively deterred and checked by the costs of pursuing them wholeheartedly.

In the balance-of-power system, the actors maintain a system of effective countervailing power by virtue of a rough equality of their material power. In the contemporary system—economic as well as political—we see, not equivalence of power but equivalence of impotence. Therefore, deterrence, not balance, is the system's defining characteristic.

The effectiveness of deterrence in our times reflects the escalating costs of international activism. These costs are the product of fundamental factors peculiar to our times. The most obvious is the destructive power of nuclear weapons. Another is the nearly universal triumph of the principle of national self-determination as the test of political legitimacy and the political energizer of peoples, formerly passive, in defense of their own interests. A third is the rise of economic expectations. The growing pressure on national authorities of economic claims makes states less willing to accept the risks of any international activism that is much more than verbal or symbolic. In the past, the pressure of economic claims was often the source of, or at least the excuse for, imperial or hegemonial aims, as in the case of Japan and Germany in the 1930s. In our time, the pressure of economic claims on available resources is more likely to damp and thwart than to encourage the international ambitions of political leaders. Few nations today expect to solve or even to mitigate their pressing economic problems by an activist foreign policy.

These three characteristics of the contemporary international system largely explain the paradox of the impotence of power—the limited ability of nation states, even the most powerful, to make direct and efficient use of that power, be it military, technological, or economic, to serve their interests. We are familiar with this phenomenon insofar as nuclear weapons are concerned. Vietnam is the most recent lesson in the impotence of conventional military might wielded by a halfhearted giant against nationalist adversaries convinced of the rightness of their cause—and able to convince most of the world, too.

The weak response of the industrial countries to OPEC's challenge demonstrates that great economic power, too, can be ineffective against a determined challenge that has a certain appeal to the world's sense of economic justice. The industrial countries have also avoided a confrontation with OPEC because they dare not risk provoking another oil embargo—so little confidence do they have in the willingness of their dissatisfied constituents to put up with even temporary shortages and unemployment for the sake of the national interest. In short, the expectations of general prosperity and the close link between the success of governments in achieving that prosperity and their political legitimacy, greatly inhibit the adventurous use of power for radical changes in the international system.

Grand Alternatives

Discussions (including our own) of the future of the international economic system have been largely in terms of three possible modes of organization:

(1) Reestablishment of the hegemony of the United States, particularly in the monetary field.

(2) The consolidation of Western Europe into an effective economic bloc, with a substantial degree of central decision making in the field of money to match the existing centralization of policy making in external commercial policy and agriculture. This would tend to create a two-bloc system for the industrial world.

(3) A far-reaching disintegration of the international economic system along national lines—repeating what is supposed to have occurred in the early 1930s.

We might pause briefly to ask why the issue is conventionally posed in terms of these particular alternatives. The reasons are doubtless historical and ideological. Many Americans and some Europeans would like to believe that the old notion of Atlantic economic integration under the leadership of the United States is still a relevant objective; many Europeans and a few Americans still feel the same way about the idea of European economic integration. And memories of the 1930s, revived by the breakdown of fixed exchange rates between 1971 and 1973—reminiscent as it was of the breakdown of gold parities in 1931-36—may explain the present preoccupation with a scenario of general disintegration.

Then, too, the history of the international economic system since 1913 has been conventionally taught as a morality play in which the good integrationist forces struggle against the evil forces of economic nationalism, first losing in the 1930s then winning after World War II, under the benign leadership of the United States. Now, again, the same good and evil forces are seen to be in contention, although the current expectation is that this time Satan may prevail.

What these three scenarios have in common is their abstractness and their intellectual extremism. All three exclude a broad middle ground in which integrationist (both Atlantic and European) and disintegrationist forces coexist uneasily as partly realized, partly blocked tendencies in a system that is essentially stable, despite the pressure of special interests for national protection and a discordant chorus of demands for structural reform. For even those nationalist forces which block further integration are themselves sufficiently constrained to limit their disintegrating effects. Despite the strong urge to national independence unfettered by international obligations, the world economic system will remain relatively open and predominantly liberal.

The Limits of Economic Nationalism

Economic nationalism has its roots in classical mercantilism and in nineteenth-century protectionism. The former was largely concerned with the state's military power, for which the acquisition of a large stock of bullion was necessary. The latter had its origins in the middle and late 1800s in the efforts of Germany, France, and the United States to industrialize in the face of British competition, and of Continential European countries to protect their traditional agriculture from cheap food from North America, Australia, and the Argentine.

During the early 1930s, new dimensions, both economic and political, were added. As unemployment rose and prices fell, many countries at first raised tariffs. Much of the impetus came from the U.S. Tariff Act of 1930, which triggered a wave of tariff retaliation that spread rapidly around the globe. Then in 1932, after sterling fell, came a wave of nontariff restrictions.

This "new protectionism," as it was called, was mainly an attempt by Continental European countries that were unwilling to devalue their currencies to protect their international reserves, domestic money supplies, and employment from the consequences of monetary contraction and depression in the United States. The countries that clung to their old gold parities after the two leading currencies had been depreciated were those that made the most extensive use of import quotas, export subsidies and, in Germany's case, multiple exchange rates and bilateral clearing. In the case of Germany, Italy, and Japan, there was also a military motive: to reduce vulnerability to blocade in the event of a war of attrition with the democracies.

Significantly, the reaction against trade barriers on the part of the Western democracies began simultaneously with the decision of France and the other gold bloc countries to devalue in 1936. The Tripartite Agreement of that year contains what was, I believe, the first major international declaration of intent "without delay to relax and progressively remove the present system of quotas and exchange controls with a view to their abolition."

The economic nationalism of the 1930s, then, was associated with the division of the industrial world into hostile ideological camps, with the Great Depression and with the attempts of Continental European countries to maintain the forms of the gold standard after its substance had been radically transformed by the fall of sterling and the devaluation of the dollar.

I have reviewed this familiar history in order to remind us of fundamental differences between then and now. The industrial countries no longer have significant military or security reasons to impose trade barriers. On the contrary, to the extent that trade barriers cause its resources to be used less efficiently, a nation's power to prepare for war may be reduced. And given the present state of military technology and political relations among the industrial countries (they constitute a "security community" under the nuclear umbrella of the United States), there is clearly no need to prepare for a war of attrition.

Moreover, the contemporary, normally expansive and inflationary world monetary climate, as well as the flexibility of exchange rates among major currencies, are not particularly conducive to the imposition of trade barriers. At least they are far less so than the deflationary climate and fixed gold parities of the early 1930s.

In a deflationary climate, import restrictions, controls on capital outflows, and the deliberate undervaluation of the currency are tempting, because these measures can have, in the short run, a positive impact on employment. They are also likely to provoke retaliation—the more so because it is considered unconscionable for a country to try to export unemployment. In an expansive, inflationary climate, a country is not tempted to restrict imports of goods and services but rather to restrict imports of capital. For restrictions on imports of goods tend to raise domestic prices, while restrictions on capital imports tend to hold prices down (by holding down the domestic money supply). For the same reason, countries are more inclined to try to overvalue than undervalue their currencies; witness the intervention policies of Britain, Italy, and Japan in 1974. Such measures are also unlikely to provoke retaliation or offsetting measures by other countries. Although they amount in principle to an attempt to export inflation, the effect on other countries is diffuse—and surely less damaging in welfare terms—than the effect of attempts to export unemployment under conditions of general deflation.

Moreover, the power of vested interests in maintaining the openness of international markets is greater today than in the interwar period, when the world was innocent of the experience of trade warfare. Today, memories of the 1930s stand as a warning that immoderate restriction of trade and competitive exchange-rate policies do not work because they are sure to provoke general retaliation.

In the industrial world at least, the nation-states have been tamed in their economic as in their political relations.

The form of the nation-state, including its traditional apparatus of legal rights is preserved, even universalized, yet its substance is transformed. The old boy is still there, but he has lost much of his vigor and bite. The present international system removes simultaneously the incentives to madness and to merger. Nations are economically interdependent enough not to indulge in the kinds of suicidal policies that marked the national responses to the great depression of the 1930s, yet they are not so interdependent as to be forced to break out of their national shells, or able to disrupt the world through isolated acts of autarchy. They are militarily interdependent enough to be well aware of the ever-present peril of annihilation in a world without hiding places. Thus, through the cunning of History (one dare not call it Reason), the kind of world Wilson dreamed about emerges in circumstances that would have given him nightmares.[2]

Tamed as the nation-states may be, however, they remain for the foreseeable future sufficiently strong to block further international integration. Hence the structural stability of our untidy international monetary system.

The Frustration of Monetary Reform

Perhaps the most compelling evidence of the structural stability of the existing international economic order is the frustration of international monetary reform. No subject in the realm of international economic policy has aroused more interest—or passion—or engaged more talent and energy. A bewildering array of plans and proposals, a library of official reports, tens of thousands of man-hours of international negotiation, but all to virtually no avail. The international monetary system has evolved, to be sure, *de facto* from a fixed-rate dollar standard to a dollar standard with somewhat greater flexibility of rates, at least among major currencies. But for all the official effort, there is hardly anything to show.

The fundamental reasons are (1) that the existing system corresponds rather precisely to the present balance of monetary power between the United States and the other important nations, Germany, France, Britain, and Japan; and (2) that none of the nations is willing to take important risks to try to force a major change. De Gaulle went as far as he could—or dared—in the 1960s, with his rather halfhearted gold-purchase policy. The result was not to advance France's stated objective of a symmetrical system, more like the classical gold standard, but to hasten the advent of a naked dollar standard, without even the fig leaf of nominal convertibility of the dollar into gold.

In the most recent phase of negotiations on monetary reform, which began in 1972, both sides agreed that the aim was greater symmetry, or equality. To officials in the United States, this meant mainly greater exchange-rate flexibility, in the sense that the United States would be as able as other countries to use its exchange rate as an instrument of economic policy. To this end it proposed that exchange rates (assumed to be pegged rather than floating) should be adjusted according to changes in official reserves and other "objective indicators."

To some other countries, and in particular France, symmetry meant something different; namely, the gradual elimination of the dollar as an important reserve currency. This was to be accomplished by "mandatory asset settlement" or convertibility in the classical sense. All countries, including the United States, would be required to settle their official payments deficits by transferring gold, Special Drawing Rights, or foreign currencies, rather than by accumulating official claims in dollars. In this way, what de Gaulle once called the dollar's "exorbitant privilege" as a reserve currency would be eliminated.

Neither the American nor the European positions was consistent with the underlying realities of power and interest. For the United States, an active exchange-rate policy would be inconsistent with the role of the dollar as leading reserve currency—a role officials of the United States were most anxious to preserve and even strengthen, despite occasional lip service to "voluntary asset settlement."

> Despite this country's insistence on symmetry of the adjustment mechanism, and on its own freedom of action on exchange rates, in a reformed international monetary system, and despite the Federal Reserve's commitment in principle to exchange-rate intervention, under certain conditions, actual intervention by the United States has been limited. . . . The United States remains largely passive as to its exchange rates. . . . An active exchange rate policy for the United States is fundamentally inconsistent with the continued use of the dollar as a major intervention currency. [3]

The European position was hardly more realistic or consistent. A system that mandated asset settlement, and which would also maintain reasonable stability of exchange rates, would presuppose close coordination of monetary policies among the principal powers. Under the classical gold standard, it is taught, the free market provided the coordination of monetary conditions necessary to maintain fixed exchange rates. In today's world, governments and central banks are expected to manage demand in an effort to avoid the traumatic dislocations that are associated with the gold standard in the popular mind. Hence, deliberate coordination of national monetary policies would be required to make convertibility in the classical sense possible again. In present conditions, convertibility might even require something close to a supranational monetary authority, with power to control the expansion of the world's monetary base by means of its control of the creation of international reserve assets (SDRs). No country, France least of all, was prepared to accept any such radical abridgment of its monetary autonomy. It must be assumed that the European demand for mandatory asset settlement was no more serious than the demand the United States made for freedom to pursue an active exchange-rate policy.

Despite the frustration of monetary reform, the greater flexibility of exchange rates between the dollar and other leading currencies has improved the system—marginally at least—in both economic and political terms. It has eliminated the disruptive monetary effects of massive central bank intervention in support of fixed parities, when currencies are under speculative pressure. And it softens the conflicts of interest between the United States and European countries over monetary and exchange-rate policies, while giving the larger countries an opportunity to pursue somewhat more autonomous domestic monetary policies.

Still, these changes are of limited importance. The system still suffers from currency speculation, though it now affects exchange rates more than domestic monetary aggregates. Witness the gyrations of the DM/dollar rate over the last two years. Such gyrations can have damaging effects on domestic prices and the competitive position of export and import-competing industries. And partly for this reason, most countries have been unwilling—or politically unable—to take advantage of the greater monetary autonomy which exchange-rate flexibility makes possible, at least for larger countries.

The international monetary system, then, remains essentially as it was in the 1960s with an inconvertible dollar standard, though with a little more exchange-rate flexibility. I see nothing that would basically alter that structure in the foreseeable future. A European monetary union, with centralized control of the members' monetary bases, could accomplish such a change. But the present system probably works well enough to rule that possibility out. The emergent Continental

European currency bloc, led by Germany, with exchange rates fixed or relatively stable among the members' currencies, shelters the members from the worst feature of the present wider system—the instability of the exchange rate between the mark and the dollar. This development makes more likely the indefinite persistence of the present system.

Rich Nations and Poor Nations

If structural change can be made in the international economic order, it will be made in the relations between the industrial countries and certain developing countries. Yet even here change will be limited by the inability of developing countries to mobilize sufficient economic power—either because, oil apart, they lack monopoly control of anything that is hard for the industrial countries to do without, or because they are deterred by fear of retaliation from using what power they may have.

Apart from sovereign control over a few vital materials that are scarce in the industrial countries, the Third World has one important asset in the game of international economic politics: its poverty. The asset is moral and psychological rather than material; it is valuable nonetheless. OPEC's unexpected success in maintaining a solid front on oil prices and in dividing its powerful opponents was due in large part to the members' conviction of the justice of their cause. This conviction removed the enterprise from the category of a cartel, a power game, or an exhibition of economic greed, and transfigured it into a revolt of the poor against the rich. The interpretation is not without its ironies. "Poor" oil sheiks are taking from poor Indians as well as from rich Americans and Europeans. Nevertheless, the success of OPEC in attracting political support even from their poorer victims (witness the pro-Arab majorities in the United Nations General Assembly) as well as (much more ambivalently) from public opinion in

Europe and North America testifies to the importance of this moral dimension. History and ideology have prepared the ground for this strange twist. The legacy of anticolonialism, the Marxist notion of an international class struggle, and, as Daniel P. Moynihan recently pointed out, British Fabian Socialism all contributed.[4] The result is to strengthen the hands of poor nations against rich nations, wherever the issue can be made to appear as a simple matter of redistributive justice.

It is hardly surprising, then, that the issue of the terms of trade between industrial and developing countries has achieved such prominence in thought and action. Twenty years ago, Raúl Prebisch, the Argentine economist turned economic spokesman for the developing world, elaborated a quasi-Marxist theory of international exploitation that stressed the unfavorable terms of trade suffered by developing countries in their exchange with industrial countries. Since then, the ideology of the terms of trade has played a large and growing role in the politics of economic relations between the industrial and developing worlds. It underlies not only moves to raise raw materials prices but also the demand for one-way tariff concessions—a demand which the industrial nations have in principle accepted.

Justice not charity, trade not aid, are the rallying cries of the poor nations against the rich. And the rich nations feel under a moral compulsion to respond, at least symbolically and in principle. How far they will actually go is problematic, however. It depends not only on the conviction of poor nations of the rightness of their cause and their ability to touch the conscience of the industrial world, but also on sheer bargaining power. In the realm of economic power politics, their position is hardly strong. Apart from their control of oil, some of the metals and the tropical foodstuffs, their economic power is extremely limited. Their political capacity for common action is also limited by their cultural and political differences and their geographical dispersion. And the more advanced developing countries, such as Brazil, Mexico, Argentina, and some of the countries of the Pacific rim, suffer some of the same inhibitions on the use of economic force as the advanced industrial countries. Because they are further along the road to industrial status, they are also more aware of their dependence on open international markets.

Little OPECs and other surprises, too, may be in store. But it seems unlikely that developments between the rich and poor nations will greatly alter the broad picture of structural stability of the international economic order, in the decade or so ahead.

Notes

[1] Stanley Hoffmann, *Gulliver's Troubles* (New York, 1968), pp. 52, 54.

[2] Stanley Hoffmann, op. cit., p. 42.

[3] Marina von N. Whitman, "The Current and Future Role of the Dollar: How Much Symmetry?" *Papers on Economic Activity No. 3* (Washington, D.C.: Brookings Institution, 1974), p. 780.

[4] Daniel P. Moynihan, "The United States in Opposition," *Commentary* (March 1975), p. 31.

SYSTEMS OF INTERNATIONAL ECONOMIC ORGANIZATION

Charles P. Kindleberger

Introduction

Classical international economics made a sharp distinction between the theory of domestic prices, which were determined by the respective labor content of commodities, and of international prices determined by a different principle, the theory of comparative advantage. The basis of this difference was allegedly that labor moves freely within but not between countries. Something of the same discontinuity is found in political science between national and international politics. In national politics, government is the instrument for reconciling many differences between particular interests and for seeking the national interest. In the absence of international government, conflicts of national interest are reconciled by international relations among sovereign states, more or less constrained by international law, including treaties and agreements, and by some limited international organizations.

15

Apart from these, no instrument or institution takes the international interest as its own. I recently heard a prominent member of the Congress express his indignation on the subject of a piece of legislation which would give the president of the United States the power to take certain action on such a vague basis as the "international interest."

In an economy where no individual household or firm has power to affect prices, and prices reflect social as well as private marginal costs, the action of each individual (including firms) in maximizing his or her economic interest maximizes the interest of all. Each gain takes place without inflicting loss on others, and hence moves in the direction of Pareto optimality. This is the world of Adam Smith's invisible hand. Government's role is restricted to keeping order and the peace. There is in this system no room for the fallacy of composition, whereby one gains at the expense of others, and all by seeking so to gain leave the total worse off. There is no game theory either zero-sum, where one man's gain is another's loss, or non-zero sum, where both can gain by cooperating or lose by competing because individual actions are interdependent. And there are no public goods (apart from order, national defense, and peace) where one man's consumption does not affect the amount available for others.

In the international economy, it has long been recognized that the world of the benign invisible hand does not obtain. Unlike the households and firms of the national economy, countries in the international economy and especially in the international polity have power. A country can improve its terms of trade, that is get imports cheaper, by imposing a tariff on goods bought abroad. It can enrich itself by taking over the rich gains from trade with colonies or exotic far-away lands. The fallacy of composition argues that if each country tries to gain at the expense of others, all lose, so that it is useful to simulate the world of the invisible hand by commitments to the rule of free trade and the gold standard. Even Adam Smith believed the Navigation Laws to be a domestic public good because they provided national defense—a good he held to be of greater importance than opulence (though a recent paper suggests he was being ironic in this thought), and allowed room for game-theoretic considerations in advocating tariffs for bargaining purposes.

It seems clear that Adam Smith underestimated the contribution which English mercantilism, embodied in the Navigation and Stapling Acts, and export and import taxes and prohibitions, made not just to defense but to English commercial expansion in the seventeenth and early eighteenth centuries. Indeed, they contributed powerfully to the industrial revolution and British economic ascendency in the world. In the view of Friedrich List, free trade is the clever device of the climber who kicks away the ladder when he has attained the summit of greatness, rather than the economic rule which counsels economic self-restraint in the interests of all participants.

Europe did move to practice free trade from 1820 to 1875 under British ideological leadership. The movement can be interpreted variously as altruistic, each country loving its neighbors as itself; as self-interested, each country, however, acting in its long-run self-interest; as the application of generalized rules of self-restraint, conditional on the agreement of others in the interest of the system and of the separate countries; as a system of alliances interacting with one another; or as the result of the leadership of one country, dominating or at least leading the international system in what it perceived as the international interest.

These possible explanations: altruism, long-run interests, generalized functional rules and institutions, regional blocs, and leadership make up the five bases of international economic organization to be discussed. There is a sixth: world government, which is not treated on the ground that to do so would be premature by several decades. We further omit the treatment of planned systems, like that of COMECON and the problems of the interaction between planned trade of the

Sino-Soviet type and Western market systems. Utopianism is an excuse which does not perhaps apply here, and it is recognized that more than one voice has been raised recently in favor of national and international planning, but the content of this discussion at the international level is minimal.

From one point of view, generalized rules and institutions embrace a variety of subsystems based on functional and regional groupings. The leadership system has subvariants as well: dominance, leadership, leadership of an alliance, balance-of-power strategy, and so on. Mixtures are possible such as regional blocs with dominant leadership. All are discussed in light of the assumption that the world economy is subject to game-theoretic interaction, including the fallacy of composition yielding a negative-sum game, and that there is an international interest, if only the public good of peace in the purely political field, and stability and growth in the economic. Each system, moreover, is subject to entropy or decay—so much so, indeed, that, as in bureaucratic organization, changing back and forth among systems may be more satisfactory than choosing and sticking to one. But the transitions are fraught with instability.

Altruism

Self-interest works satisfactorily when no unit has power. But Christian and other philosophies of altruism admit power implicitly into their systems by recommending loving one's neighbors as one's self.

Altruism explains some actions in international relations, such as the readiness of small countries—Canada, Sweden, Switzerland, and New Zealand among others—to take a prominent role in supplying troops to U.N. forces, and in providing foreign aid to a much greater extent, in relation to their national income, than larger, more wealthy nations. From one point of view, of course, these actions are based on self-interest; the country in question wishes to maximize an objective function which includes the image of itself as a paragon of behavior in a world of self-seeking nations. For the most part, however, altruism can be interpreted as serving long-run self-interests. A country contributes to the international public good of peace keeping because of its lively appreciation of the importance of avoiding war, which, starting anywhere, might spread, and disrupt even if it did not engulf the world. Altruism and long-run self-interest are the equivalent of the Categorical Imperative of Emmanuel Kant, which calls for the individual or nations to act only in ways which can be generalized. They are the opposite of the position of the "free rider," who gets by with his actions only because others are providing the public goods needed by the system.

The economic theory of public goods hypothesizes that they are underproduced because of free riding. The title of a well-known paper on the subject by two political scientists is "I Get Along with a Little Help from My Friends." Another popular view of the subject is embodied in the expression "Let George do it." Free riding in international politics is illustrated by the small country which belongs to NATO but maintains no national defense force. A small amount of free riding is tolerable in the system, provided that sufficient public goods are produced by someone. But, unfortunately, the temptation to free ride is omnipresent, and when some critical number or proportion of countries yield to it, the production for the public good ceases. Small countries which resist free riding may be said to be altruistic, or if they are conscious that their marginal importance as participants is positive, self-interested in the long-run rather than the short-run sense. Altruism may be embodied in informal rules (the formal we come to presently); I have written about my cynical English friend before when I cited his indignation that rats should be criticized for abandoning the sinking ship; he also enjoys the remark of the man who said he preferred going on a cruise on the ships of ——— nationality where they had none of that nonsense about women and children into the lifeboats first. Altruism is to be welcome in the international economy for serving as an example—if not for the self-satisfaction it affords its practitioners. The pressure of self-interest, however, particularly on the poor, but, in trying times, on any country, makes altruism unsatisfactory as a basis for a generalized system.

Enlightened Self-Interest

We should likewise be skeptical of basing our system on enlightened self-interest, with which altruism is intimately connected, for much the same set of reasons as given above. The good is the enemy of the necessary in some circumstances. High rates of time preference may make it impossible for the poor to forego a small gain today for a larger one in the future. A bird in the hand is worth one-plus in the bush, etc. Even when budget restraints, rates of interest, and uncertainty do not oblige a country to opt for short-run gains, myopic greed leading to irrationality may. Sheik Yamani, if we are to believe the press, argued for a smaller increase in the price of oil which would not evoke defensive and retaliatory responses from consuming countries; but he was voted down by other members of OPEC. In the case of Venezuela with dwindling reserves, the calculation may be a rational one. Other members may prove to have miscalculated.

Different rules should probably apply to large countries than to small. The small country has no power to affect the international interest except by example and this may escape notice; the extent of its participation will not determine whether some or another public good is provided or not. Its action in its short-run economic interest is likely to have no feedback, no impact on the action of others. The short-term actions of large countries do have consequences however.

They are prominent and their national income, foreign trade, foreign-exchange reserves, and the like have foreign repercussions. They are price makers, rather than price takers, in Metzler's memorable phrase.

Between the most prominent large country with responsibility to act in the long-run interest, since its size and power used for short-run advantage are likely to inflict cost on others, and the small country with no power and no responsibility, there are two awkward cases. When a number of small countries, each acting to protect itself, move in parallel, the total effect may prove dysfunctional. An example I have used elsewhere is the separate actions of Belgium, Holland, and Switzerland in converting sterling to gold in the summer of 1931, while France, a middle power with large sterling holdings, refrained from exerting pressure on the pound, and in fact joined the Federal Reserve Bank of New York in providing loans. The withdrawal of any one of these small countries would have been supportable; those of all three were not. (It could be argued, perhaps, that the long-run interest of all countries were best served by the depreciation of sterling, but this changes the nature of the issue under discussion.) In the next phase, the three countries plus France converted dollars into gold and exerted strong deflationary pressure on the United States from September 21, 1931, until the passage of the Glass-Steagall bill in February 1932. The weak acting in concert are strong, as the Fascist symbol reminds us, but it is hard to criticize this last would-be free rider.

The other and more difficult case involves the middle power that possesses insufficient strength to lead the system, and hence is without responsibility, but has enough power to be a spoiler. Thus, the cooperation of the small countries is not necessary to support a given system—though in the light of what straws can do, it may be advisable. On the other hand, that of middle powers like France may well be essential. Middle-power views do not, of course, inevitably converge with those of large powers. The middle power may argue that a certain course of action is called for in the public international interest—return to the gold standard, for example—when larger powers consider that this is not in the long-run interest (though it may appear that larger powers primarily perceive it is not in their short-run interest). The result is impasse. Or the middle power may proceed to pursue its short-run interest at some risk to the public good of international stability or peace-keeping—converting dollars to gold in 1965, selling Mirages to the Arabs, or making its own deals in oil independently of the consortium of consumers. Some power, and claims to but not possession of responsibility, may lead the middle power to pursue its own version of the public international interest at one moment, its private national interest at another.

Even when all countries pursue what they believe to be their long-run interest because of their enlightenment, it is by no means clear that their paths converge. Or if we define long-run interest as a goal consonant with the actions of others, it is not certain that such a self-interest will exist. We turn on this account to the question of living by rules, which may be taken to embody a system congruent with the long-run public interest.

An International Economy Managed by Rule

Leon Fraser, first president of the Bank for International Settlements, used to complain that while he heard interminable discussion of the rules of the gold-standard game, he never saw them written down. Recent research, moreover, has made it clear that the gold standard of the second half of the nineteenth century was a continuously evolving, somewhat ambiguous mechanism of adjustment, with room for play and for *ad hoc* intervention. The point is that even under systems of rule there may be difficulties: first in agreeing on explicit rules or on the content of the implicit rules, and second in their application to particular cases.

The rules may be broad statements of principle which are given content by a common-law procedure, or an explicit and detailed statement of rights and duties under specified conditions. More important than the character of the rules and agreements, in my judgement, is unity of thought and purpose behind them. Adroit draftsmanship can paper cracks with forms of words to which parties to an agreement give different meaning. Such agreements are not worth a great deal. Illustrations are the Potsdam Agreement of August 1945, the United Nations Declaration on Human Rights, and the draft charter of the International Trade Organization. Provision for broad principles and specific exceptions yield a meaningless result as one party fastens on principles and the other on exceptions. The draft ITO charter was rejected by the United States Senate, or rather not taken up, because in effect it legislated exceptions to the principles of reduced duties and nondiscriminatory trade, providing as it did exceptions for full employment, balance-of-payments difficulties, countries in early stages of growth and development, and the like.

Makers of rules and institutions may be myopic. The International Monetary Fund and the World Bank were too small to handle the postwar reconstruction problem, which required a Marshall plan on an *ad hoc* basis, and the assumption underlying the IMF that international capital movements could and should not be revived and could be contained by exchange controls proved wide of the mark as well. The foreign-exchange theory underlying the IMF par-value system has also been criticized as archaic, though I reserve my position on that issue. Purposes may be agreed upon, but their implementation in rules may be faulty.

Or rules may be agreed upon but not put into action as countries refrain from applying them for fear that not enough other countries will follow. The League of Nations study, *Commercial Policy in the Interwar Period*, regarded it as a striking paradox that between 1927 and 1929 the countries of Europe consistently agreed to lower tariffs, all the while raising them. It concluded that governments were prepared collectively to advocate policies which implied trust to some limited extent, but were unwilling to act on the basis of such trust. Assume congruent ends, and intelligent rules. Some country under some provocation or circumstances will want to break them. There may be provision for enforcement, perhaps in sanctions against the violator. But even if free riders do not erode the rules, entropy may do so. The par-value rules of the IMF were nodded to perfunctorily by the British in their devaluation of 1949 and entirely ignored shortly thereafter by Canada when it adopted floating. Rules are not always dropped merely because they are easy to ignore. Even when the rule is clear and applicable, there may be difficulty in applying it. Sanctions against Italy in 1936 and Rhodesia in the 1960s provide cases in point. Where the police are politically opposed to a rule, or to its application in a given case, or where application is expensive, there may be free riding in the application of sanctions. In the Ethiopian case in 1936 as recited by Herbert Feis, it was easy to stop the large American oil companies from delivering oil to Italy, but single tanker operators sprang into the vacuum created and delivered oil to Italy at railheads in Eritrea in profusion.

Rules and institutions also come to be ignored from the tendency of the regulator over time to identify with rather than repress the interest it has been created to provide surveillance over. Thus, no American official who was a country committee member in the Marshall Plan administration wanted less rather than more aid for "his country." Functional organizations of the United Nations in aircraft, meteorology, food and agriculture, labor, health, and the like each now wants more rather than less attention to the problem it addresses. The World Bank provides loans to *all* developing members, like prizes at a children's party, without being permitted to formulate an iron-clad allocation rule such as loans to the poorest, loans where they will produce the most growth, or where the financial chances of repayment are best. (Regional banks, created alongside the World Bank, in effect guarantee that indiscriminate policy by ensuring that funds will not be reallocated from one continent to another where they might be more useful.) Assume a system of functional rules and institutions: IBRD and IMF for international lending and international monetary questions; GATT and UNCTAD for trade; ILO for labor; OECD for aid, statistics, some coordination of macroeconomic policy, and some international corporate problems; the United Nations special commission for other (and the same) problems of international investment; the Bank for International Settlements, Group of Ten, Committee of Twenty also in monetary affairs, with links to the IMF and the OECD, not to mention the ECE, ECAFE, and other regional commissions of the UN, and EEC, ICAO, FAO, WHO, UNESCO, the Pan American Union and the like. How are these to be coordinated? One possibility would be to have them sorted out through the Economic and Social Council of the United Nations, and this is nominally done for many organizations. There are direct links among many pairs and triangles of agencies. The IMF and GATT, for example, together decide in particular cases whether restrictions in imports are protective in character or fall under the heading of exchange control.

A further complication is that two or more countries may choose to ignore the international machinery altogether. In this they may or may not decide to be bound by the rules governing an international agency. In the world of national sovereignties, the strength of international institutions, their innovative capacity, and their dedication in formulating and applying consistent standards of conduct depends on the member governments, and more on the larger than on the smaller ones. A high official of the International Monetary Fund said in my presence nearly ten years ago, and the date is important, that when the United States did not push for particular action in the IMF nothing happened. The United

Nations has lately been taken over by the developing countries, which are formulating statements, adopted with large majorities by the General Assembly, on programs of action in international aid problems of raw materials and development, a declaration for the establishment of a new international economic order, the permanent sovereignty of every state over its natural resources, to establish a commission for dealing with problems of international investment, and the like. Like the United Nations Commission on Trade and Development, these efforts represent the views of a large majority of the countries of the world by number, but only a small minority in terms of economic indicators such as national income, international trade, production of manufactured goods and the like. (Since October 1973 this small minority has become stronger obviously by a quadrupling of the price of oil.)

A meeting of minds on such questions as the control of raw-material cartels, international commodity planning, international investment, foreign aid, linking international monetary issues to foreign aid, tariff preferences for developing countries and the like is certainly distant. Even in the IMF, where voting is weighted to reflect wealth, 20 per cent of the votes can block action, and hence stalemate is assured. Formerly, the United States alone had a veto. Then Western Europe acquired one when and if the enlarged European Economic Community voted together, as France insists it should and must. Now the "uncommitted nations" led by India have pieced together a bloc which will forestall action unless new votes of Special Drawing Rights are accompanied by special issues to provide resources to the (free riding) developing countries. With three groups able to veto, stalemate is inevitable. As a further example, in the United Nations Assembly, numerous votes might be cast by a majority that is becoming populist, but unless there is a meeting of minds which includes the richer developed members, nothing will happen there either. Democracy in international political and economic organizations is meaningless unless it is based on a community of views. The point came home to me first on the occasion of the UNRRA meeting of August 1945. There were seventeen members of the UNRRA council, each with a vote. At that time, the United States had proposed a second $2,750,000,000 tranche of UNRRA to provide relief and rehabilitation to Allied nations. In the first tranche, the United States had furnished 72 percent of the aid, Britain 12, Canada 6, the Soviet Union 2, if I recall the figures correctly. Canada chose to give aid directly to Britain, and withdrew—not perhaps a free rider, but a rider headed east rather than north, with a different objective than the international interest generally. Britain stated it was unwilling to vote a second tranche unless Italy and Austria, for which it provided 50 percent of Allied relief, were charged to the UNRRA rolls. This reduced the aid available to other countries, but relieved the hard-pressed United Kingdom. The Soviet Union was a (nominal) contributor to international aid, out of pride, though it would have been entitled to have been a recipient on the basis of need. It was prepared to vote for the second tranche of UNRRA only on the proviso that two countries it knew to be in need, Byelo-Russia and the Ukraine, were added to the list of recipients. In the absence of agreed principles for dealing with foreign aid—and the search for such principles continues today after three decades—the international institution degenerated to logrolling; the United States was saddled with the burden of providing international relief, and this country moved, in the Marshall Plan and Point IV, to bilateral assistance. In time, according to a widespread view, bilateral aid in turn degenerated from a charitable to a foreign-policy enterprise.

To sum up, an international system of institutions and rules provides for solving problems in the international economic system, but unless these rules are widely recognized as legitimate, internalized, and probably applied by the pressure of one or more leading countries on various organizations in a coordinated way, the system is still subject to frustration because short-run maximizers defy the rules, free riders ignore them when they cost anything, and the bureaucrats are often incapable of running the machinery of the institutions to overcome the resistance inherent in conflicts of interests.

Regional Blocs

The suggestion has frequently been made that the international polity, and economy, be organized into regional blocs at the first stage above the national. It also has been suggested that relations among these few blocs at the world level would be simpler than those that are formed in the universal membership organizations open to all sovereign states large and small. The merit in the idea stems from the need for a sense of participation, and the optimum social unit in which this sense can be developed is much smaller than the optimum economic unit, which for many purposes is the world. An individual, firm or country would have a stronger sense of participation on the continental, than on the world, level and would on that account feel less anomie in a world organized by regional blocs.[1]

The European Economic Community was conceived not as a regional bloc to confront other regional blocs, but as a confederation which would adopt unified economic policies for the area and emerge as an integrated economic unit, like the United States, with greatly increased weight. In due course it became evident that harmonized policies and a sense of participation were insufficient to assure the success of a bloc. There was a need for policy-making machinery, i.e., government. Today, the question is asked whether or not organizations like the European Commission at Brussels, the Council wherever it meets, and the Parliament at Strasbourg are sufficient to constitute a government. It seems clear that they are not.

Power continues to reside in nation-states. The Commission may propose, France and Germany dispose. Moreover, the community of interests is minimal. The public EEC good is of small account compared with the private good of France, Britain, Germany, Italy or any of the others, even in EEC matters. The solution to the agricultural question is a compromise among national interests, not a solution in the general EEC interest. Regional assistance is thought of not in the abstract but with the concrete problems of Brittany, the Mezzogiorno, East Bavaria, Scotland, and Northern Ireland in mind. On many issues—national defense, monetary reform, relations with the former colonies in Africa—Germany, Britain, and the Netherlands favor an Atlantic solution, France a Franco-European one.

Econometrics has a concept of decomposable and nondecomposable matrices. Similarly, in a book on biology some years ago Caryl Haskins wrote of decomposable groups of animals like flocks of birds and packs of wolves, and of separate animals, which are organized in nondecomposable groups, like bees that die if they lose their queen with insufficient warning, or Portugese men-of-war. Any federation or confederation is presumably decomposable, whereas true integration presumably is not or at least not without the trauma of civil war or other disruptions. Distinguishing between them is tricky. In a recent paper on financial centers, I puzzled why the financial capital should be the same as the administrative capital in England, France, Germany, but in Italy, Switzerland, Canada, the United States, and Australia. A distinguished Australian economic historian suggested that the last five countries were federations which maintained local powers long after unification, resulting in a very slow unification in Canada and Australia before a single financial center dominated. He expressed the opinion that the process would be at least equally slow in the European Economic Community.

This apparent diversion into economic and political integration is not beside the point. If regional blocs could really become integrated economic and political units, and provide an adequate basis for the participation of the various members and effective machinery in decision making, they might avoid the dangers of decomposition. The process of federations evolving into integrated units, however, is time-consuming. Moreover, most blocs have primarily been vehicles for expressing the opinions of bloc leaders—the United States in North and South America, France, perhaps, or Germany in Europe. The bloc system will be undemocratic if workable; more likely, it will simply be unworkable.[2]

But, assume that there were a "natural leader" in each bloc, prepared to suppress its private national interest in the interest of the bloc and leading in the short run more or less by consent. This is a strong but perhaps not contrary-to-fact assumption in ordinary times, although it is clearly contrary to fact as regards the United States (and France) today. Whatever its economic aspects, and I find them less than appealing, such a system of blocs is politically unattractive. A country like Canada wants a counterweight to the United States, its elephantine neighbor. When Britain was up to it, Canada liked to balance between Britain and the United States. With Britain weakened, it looked about to China or Latin America for a new counterpoise to the United States. Australia and New Zealand long relied on Britain. When that relationship lost its supportive quality, and, for example, Australia was eased out of the London capital market, Australia turned to the United States. The fact that the United States could not decide the question of admitting Australian meat and wool caused the Australians to develop ties with Japan and the Far East, particularly Indonesia. The economic orphaning of New Zealand when Britain joined the European Common Market is a story difficult to recount without emotion. Uruguay and Argentina are natural trade and investment partners with Europe, not the United States. Israel hardly belongs in a Middle East bloc.

For many reasons, a country's economic interests stretch round the world. As a result, Saudi Arabia may join a Japanese,

European, or American bloc, and so it must consider whether or not it should align its money in a world of flexible exchange rates with the dollar, mark, yen, or the Lebanese riyal. Mexico borrows in Frankfurt and the London Euro-dollar market as well as in New York. One could multiply examples endlessly. (For example, it might be politically advantageous to limit multi-national corporations to exclusive regions in some few cases, but it is hard to think of them. Latin America welcomes the competition of Japanese and European firms; East Asia does not want to be the province of Japan alone. Japan and Europe want investment by American technological leaders.)

In short, the regional-bloc notion fails to take account of the world scale of economic issues. It would add to problems rather than abate them. The European Economic Community will strengthen world economic organization when it ultimately becomes an economic and political unit, which is far from the case today. The complications added by the present organization may be tolerable for the security and the benefits in specialization it has brought to the area. It is an expedient, however, not usefully elevated into a principle.

Leadership

I come last to the principle of organization based on leadership. It is easy to detect in the order of the discussion an ancient debating device: to list a long line of alternatives, shoot down all but the last, and to point to that as the only possible course of action because others failed. My view is at the same time more scientific and more cynical. It is more scientific because I am not putting forward the leadership principle in a normative light but in a positive one. It is cynical because the leadership principle is subject to entropy too. If the internationsl system does not form integral communities (which are more often united against an external enemy than bound by positive interests) with a single decision-making apparatus chosen and perpetuated by means held to be legitimate and even sanctified, the system tends to adopt leadership. Where public goods are provided by accepted government, they emanate from a leader.

In the nineteenth century, Britain was the leader of the world economic system. Sterling was international money. The public goods consisted of a market for distress goods, provided by British free trade; a countercyclical flow of capital, produced by the City of London; coordination of macroeconomic policies and exchange rates provided by the rules of the gold standard, legitimized and internationalized by usage; a leader of last resort in the Bank of England, after the Bank Act of 1844 was suspended in crisis.

The United States took over leadership after World War II. The nineteenth-century formula of the gold standard, free trade, and budgets balanced annually had broken down, and after depression and war the United States led a drive for international rules and institutions: tariff reduction and nondiscriminatory trade would be managed by an International Trade Organization; capital movements for development by the World Bank; international monetary relations by the par-value system of currencies, and repayable credits based on quotas geared to trade by the IMF. Ostensibly, the system was to be organized by rules and international institutions. In reality, it was led by the United States.

America pushed hard for the elimination of quotas and advocated tariff reductions universally, but it tolerated foot dragging by Europe and Japan. As Japanese growth soared and exports poured out, the United States accepted a disproportionate share. The World Bank started out by using dollars exclusively, both from the American quota and from government-guaranteed loans raised in the United States. The Bank did so because the international monetary standard was based on the dollar, not gold. Other countries could change the price of their currencies in relation to the dollar, and did so from

1949 onward. They could not change the price of gold. The United States could change the price of gold, and did not until 1971, but it could not change the price of the dollar. The asymmetry of the system was perceived only slowly, except perhaps by President de Gaulle. After capital markets opened up in 1958, Europe and Japan could add to their dollar reserves by borrowing. This involved borrowing long (or selling existing companies to United States firms) and lending short. It added abundant liquidity to the system despite fears of some economists that the world was short, or potentially short, of liquidity. The same effect was achieved unintentionally by failing to understand that capital markets were joined and that on that account, national monetary policies were no longer independent. When the United States tried to lower interest rates, or West Germany or Japan to raise them, dollars poured abroad for the long or short term on private account and had to be recycled by monetary authorities, this despite strenuous efforts by the United States from 1963 on to limit its foreign lending.

Thus did American leadership decay. A glance at the little book edited by Carlo Cipolla, *The Decline of Empires*, is persuasive that the phenomenon is not new. The cause is usually a combination of war and inner decay. War of course can stimulate, as it did for the United States in two world wars, but not the war in Vietnam. Five wars—three against Britain and two against France—did in the Dutch Empire by 1730 or so. British economic world leadership was not put down after World War I; it slipped and fell. Some time after 1968, the United States was aching to escape from burdens of leadership. By August 1971 it had dumped them.

Shortly after World War II, François Perroux, the French economist, developed a theory called the domination effect. Domination was said to exist when any action of A affected B, but none of B's action required adaptation in A. Domination can occur in countries, among firms in an industry, among intellectuals in a social group, in any sort of relationship.

Legitimacy comes to some degree from the inevitability which is based on disproportionate power. In 1960 I wrote a paper for the McCloy Commission on National Policy called for by President Eisenhower suggesting that United States' domination in international economic life had come to an end. The paper appeared only in a French version in François Perroux's journal, *Cahiers de l'ISEA*. Leadership may be based on domination; it is sometimes called "hegemonial." But legitimacy of leadership can only come from persuasion.

Leadership may also be lost if it becomes exploitive and illegitimate; if the leader, for example, mixes up the public good of maintaining the stability of the system, with the private good of buying up foreign firms or foreign resources. Or again, the leadership system may be severely tested if the leader concludes there are too many free riders, that burdens are being inadequately shared, and that it is bearing an undue share of burdens of the international public good. Thus has the United States argued it pays too much for maintaining troops in Europe, or for foreign aid, or that it runs too large a balance-of-payments deficit, suffering unemployment because of an overvalued currency caused by exchange depreciation elsewhere. More elusive is the possibility of economic "aging," the loss of economic vitality, which makes a country less ready to save, innovate, accept burdens, even work, and more desirous of living high. Britain is said to have become tired in two world wars. There is evidence, far from conclusive, that the United States too has aged and slowed down. Even if the rest of the world wanted the United States to play the role of leader, and it were willing, its capacity for discharging the responsibilities of leadership may have declined. This view, of course, assumes that leadership has economic costs on balance, rather than benefits. But whether or not the leader is destroyed in taking up his role, the stability of the system is threatened by the absence of a leader prepared to provide the public good of stability, and thought to be legitimate in the role.

The depression of 1929-1939, in my judgement, was so wide,

so deep, and so prolonged because the world economic system was in transition from British leadership to American leadership. Britain could not provide the public good of international economic stability. From 1929 to 1939 the United States refused to do so. A decade later it was forced to, and the transition was complete. The world returned to economic stability.

At the present time the world economic system is plagued with uncertainty and uneasiness. The dollar is finished as international money, but there is no clear successor, despite the Iranian and Saudi Arabian decisions to tie the riyal to the SDR. The timetable for establishing a European money is being stretched out rather than foreshortened. The SDR is trapped in the IMF stalemate of vetoes, and monetary reform under the Committee of 20 fades into the distance. Neither the mark, the yen, nor the Swiss franc is a willing candidate for international money. The recent Herstatt, Franklin, and Sindona failures raised uneasy memories of the Credit Anstalt, the Danat Bank, and the Bank of the United States even though timely national policies managed to avert a real catastrophe. Competitive exchange-rate change has been largely avoided, as have been import controls to pass from one country to another the petrodollars of the oil-exporting countries. A few but unimportant and contained beggar-thy-neighbor actions have occurred—e.g., President Nixon's export embargos on soyabeans and scrap steel, and import controls on beef. In trade and foreign exchange at least countries seem conscious of the dangers posed by the fallacy of composition.

But there is little initiative anywhere, and what there is is in the national private interest and not accepted as legitimate. On issue after issue in which the international public interest is threatened by the private national interest—the 200-mile limit for fishing, or the rule of nondiscrimination in trade, the larger powers have just about given up. They cannot take the heat of providing the public good, either abroad or at home.

A study of history suggests the positive conclusion that the collapse of American leadershp in the economic system will not be followed by a system of altruism, although altruism and enlightened self-interest have encouraged the restraint of the last few years, nor by a spate of constitution-writing which will produce a new set of rules for world trade, money, corporations, the seabed, aid, or the transfer of technology. The system will limp along until it produces in evolutionary Darwinian fashion a new system in which the rules of the game, however devised and promulgated, are asymmetrically enforced and their costs asymmetrically shared. No obvious candidate for leader exists, whether a unified Europe, a rich and growing country like Germany or Japan, a revitalized United States, or some country of energy and wealth, like Brazil, which has yet to make its presence felt on the world scene. The transition to the choice of such a leader, made implicitly rather than by an election process will be dangerous. The present restraint will be constantly jeopardized by thrusting short-run maximizers or the spread of free riding.

For the sake of completeness, it is well to mention another possibility, though intuitively I do not have high hopes for it: tripartite leadership in which, say, Germany, Japan, and the United States combine to give stability to the system by uniting their currencies by fixed exchange rates and coordinating monetary policies. Ronald McKinnon has proposed that these three countries agree not to sterilize capital flows among themselves, that is, to run their monetary policies as a unitary one, and to guide individual monetary policy by international considerations among the three. (Fiscal policy might be more idiosyncratic, to trim up or down employment.) Other countries would be invited to join by agreeing to the rules, but would be under no compulsion to do so. The public good of international stability would be provided by three countries rather than one, all sharing the inordinate cost together.[3]

The system has one critically unattractive feature. It would be interpreted as an attempt to undermine and overthrow the European Economic Community. Were Germany to coordinate its policies with the United States, it would be unable to do so with France. And Germany and France must cooperate in the interest of local European political stability. To jeopardize that cooperation in the interest of wider world stability might prove dysfunctional as instability started in Europe and spread beyond that Continent.

But whatever the abstract advantages of tripartite cooperation, Germany and Japan are not likely to be drawn to it. Both, in fact, are bemused by local national interests—private goods if you like—and do not feel themselves ready to take on wider responsibilities, even to help out the faltering United States.[4] The system would not appeal either to the Committee of 77, the group which has taken over the United Nations General Assembly and is pushing hard for Populist doctrines.

Assume, however, that the near-term resistance to the establishment of a combined leadership could be overcome. Game theory suggests that it would quickly break down. Differences of opinion would be inevitable. If each nation had a veto, stalemate would ensue. If decisions were taken by majority vote, and one country were consistently outvoted, its participation would be threatened, and the system would be likely to break down. When no country is strong enough to produce the necessary leadership, and nonhegemonial systems show little promise of producing results, a compromise system becomes more attractive. But it is doubtful that even that type of system would succeed.

Conclusion

In political terms, the provision of the world public good of economic stability is best provided, if not by a world government, by a system of rules. However, it is difficult to obtain agreement on an adequate system of such rules or the means for enforcing them. This suggests that any international economic organization based on functional rules and institutions is likely to break down. In Darwinian fashion it will be replaced by a system in which one nation serves openly or covertly as leader and is accepted as legitimate in this role by its readiness to bear a disproportionate share of the cost of providing stability, as other countries take a free ride. Even if the emergence of a leader is slow, efforts to evolve a system of rules and organizations should not be, though their success is questionable. At the least, perhaps, one can prevent the old order from disintegrating completely, even though one cannot construct a strong new one.

Americans tend to be overly impressed by the merits of constitution writing, just as the British are caught up in admiration when contemplating the evolutionary growth of law. But both require the cement of social cohesion, and when that is lacking, order cannot be produced spontaneously; it must be imposed. Benevolent despotism, as I have said before, is the best form of government because it permits us all not to pay the price of eternal vigilance. The difficulty, as noted earlier, is to keep it benevolent, or viewed as such.

Notes

[1] In the postwar period, the idea first reappeared in *The Political Economy of United States Foreign Policy*, edited by W. Y. Elliott, and largely written by H. van B. Cleveland and T. Geiger. It was explored more recently by Ernest Preeg of the National Planning Association in his *Economic Blocs and U.S. Foreign Policy*. In economic questions, more narrowly, it has been espoused by Harry G. Johnson, Robert Mundell, and numerous others, arguing, for example, for fixed exchange rates within regions, but fluctuating between blocs.

[2] Prussia, as the leader of the German Reich, first buying off the other members of the Zollverein from 1834 to 1870, and then winning its leadership role through military victory, providing an Emperor, and the adroitness of Bismarck is an exceptional case.

[3] A less ambitious proposal geographically, more so in functional

terms, is that of C. Fred Bergsten (Chapter 23 of *Toward a New International Economic Order: Selected Papers of C. Fred Bergsten, 1972-1974*, Lexington, Mass., Heath, 1975) which calls for a "bigemony," or a leadership jointly of the United States and Germany to deal with other economic issues besides exchange rates and money.

[4] An unpublished paper by Alfred Grosser has noted that German elites exhibit a "very moderate nationalism" but "without a desire for prestige or a clear will to influence directly the evolution of the international system."

THE DECLINE AND REBUILDING OF AN INTERNATIONAL ECONOMIC SYSTEM: SOME GENERAL CONSIDERATIONS

David P. Calleo

The Disintegration of the Postwar System

America, it seems, may not be the modern Rome. Indeed, the rise and fall of America's world empire may complete itself in no more than half a century. Most Americans, disclaiming imperial ambition, will not grieve much at its failure. All the same, since 1945 a large part of the world has lived within the toils of an American military, political, and economic hegemony. The passing of that hegemonial system will mean a new world and many unsettling adjustments, not least in the economic sphere.

Essentially, the American imperial system has had two rings. There has been a Near Empire and a Far Empire. In the Near Empire, an Atlantic or Pan-Atlantic Community of industrialized nations has achieved a high degree of economic integration and lived in varying degrees of dependence upon American military protection. In the Far Empire, developing countries of Latin America, the Middle East, Africa, and Asia have been tied to a different sort of American hegemony, not unlike Britain's liberal imperialism over parts of Latin America during the last century. National governments, guided by mostly indirect blandishments and pressure, have provided stable access to raw materials and investment opportunities. Imperialism, of course, need not be exploitative. Certainly, the American system has brought many benefits to its participants, particularly when compared to the likely alternatives. The Near Empire has enjoyed an unparalleled era of stable security and prosperity since World War II. America's nuclear protectorate and NATO's military arrangements have given European states an effortless security unmatched in their modern histories. American encouragement of free trade has helped European economies spark a great postwar boom. American direct investment has helped rejuvenate European industry and gradually eroded whatever advantages American technology and management enjoyed after the war. With a universal prosperity, and rapidly increasing general standards of living, Western capitalism and its bourgeoisie have seemed rejuvenated and triumphant as never before in the twentieth century. For the Near Empire, moreover, the restraints of living in an imperial system have not seemed excessive in view of its benefits. Europeans have actually been encouraged to develop a powerful economic bloc to rival the American economy. The same points can be made about Japan. The Japanese, while enjoying an unprecedented access to American markets and technology, have protected their domestic base by closely restricting foreign trade and investment. In summary, hegemony has been generous. Indeed, the very generosity of the Near Empire has, perhaps, been its undoing.

Conditions have not been so favorable for the Far Empire. With the sales of raw materials controlled by American and European dominated cartels, terms of trade have seemed unfavorable to primary producers. But a compensating flow of economic and military aid, as well as increasingly heavy direct investment, have somewhat corrected the imbalance. And investments by international corporations, attracted by cheap labor, have seemed to promise rapid industrial growth to some countries of the outer ring, a hope encouraged by the prospect of developed markets opening themselves progressively to the industrial products of the developing world.

Near and Far imperial systems have reinforced each other. In particular, easy access to raw materials and investment opportunities in the Far Empire has not only helped fuel European and Japanese prosperity but also inhibited a resurgence of their own imperial ambitions.

With all its obvious advantages, why has the imperial system apparently been disintegrating? For the past decade, a growing strain has been apparent in both rings. In the Far Empire, nationalism, economic and political, has been the principal revisionist force. While we have been content to leave national governments with nominal sovereignty, provided their economies remained open and their political style was not flagrantly offensive to Western sensibilities, the political classes of many Third World countries have come to have a more ambitious definition of national self-determination. Apologists of American intervention saw Vietnam's loss beginning the unravelling of the outer imperial system. Perhaps the unmeasured nature of American policy made the prophecy self-fulfilling. In any event, the oil crisis would seem to indicate an even more significant break in the postwar system, for oil companies are typical institutions of a liberal imperialism. In such a system, a large role for private corporations seems a more appropriate form of guidance than direct governmental intervention. But now the producers' revolution has, at least temporarily, caused the imperial cartel to be replaced by a confederal nationalist cartel. The unfavorable terms of trade in the era of American hegemony have been abruptly reversed—so abruptly indeed that the OPEC countries have themselves been compelled to give foreign aid through "recycling." This economic revolution, which some fear will spread to other commodities if allowed to prevail, constitutes a major mutation in the postwar international imperial order, a shift from an imperial to a nationalist system which may well be repeated in other parts of the system of the Far Empire, Latin America in particular.[1]

The effects of the erosion of the Far Empire reverberate strongly in Europe and Japan. At the first eruption of the oil crisis during this disintegration, it was thought that Europe and Japan would become more dependent than ever upon the United States. Now the trend seems less clear. European states, even in disarray, show some signs not only of forming a greater mutual alliance against continuing American hegemony, but also of developing an interest in extending their own bloc into a special relationship with a nationalistic Middle East.[2]

Of course, the disintegration of the Near Empire was already well underway before the oil crisis. The strain in the Pan-Atlantic system has been evident in a variety of spheres —military, diplomatic, and economic. Above all, tension has been evident in the monetary system. Thus, the financial dislocations attendant upon the oil crisis, serious as they may be, have fallen upon a monetary system already in an advanced state of disequilibrium, showing many of those symptoms of advancing disorder familiar to students of the interwar period.

The principal culprit and cause of the financial dislocations has been the United States itself. Like Britain in the 1920s, we have sought to use the dollar's status as a reserve currency to escape the normal discipline of staying in balance with the outside world. And, by exporting our surplus money, we have encouraged inflation abroad while insulating our own economy from its effects at home. During the war in Vietnam, our lack of domestic and foreign restraint became so outrageous, and the international system so overcharged, that inflation came home to roost and the disintegration of the international financial order began to accelerate.

Why should the United States have found it so difficult to maintain its external payments in balance? The causes have been both economic and political. Paradoxically, they reflect many of those factors which, in other aspects, have helped cement the imperial system. In brief, while our international corporations have carried out a massive program of foreign investment, our government has sustained a vast imperial system of foreign subsidies and military bases. The total outflow has never been balanced by an adequate inflow, even though our trade position, in itself, has generally been favorable.[3] Hence once we had expended the huge savings earned from the war, we have no longer been able to afford both our military and economic policies simultaneously. As a result, the costs of the imperial system have been financed by debt. Since the late sixties, our policy has sought equilibrium through depreciating the dollar in order to increase further the American trade surplus. Unfortunately, "dirty floats," the contemporary version of competitive devaluation, make any lasting adjustment through dollar devaluation unlikely. While we expect Germans and Japanese to play the role of the interwar gold bloc, both economies are so vulnerable to a loss of exports that their prolonged acquiescence seems unlikely. As they grow tired of supporting the dollar, they will very likely turn to protectionist blocs.[4]

In short, the international monetary system was far from equilibrium even before the shocks of the oil crisis. The consequence has been a huge piling up of surplus dollars abroad and a precipitous increase in the world's money supply. The cost of empire, therefore, has been an accelerating world inflation, perhaps already inherent in postwar capitalist societies.

As is generally true, the monetary or economic disequilibrium reflects a fundamental political imbalance. In most years, for example, our imperial military expenditures connected with the conventional military defense of Europe and Japan have in themselves equaled the basic American deficit. Our imperial system, it might be said, has not been exploitative enough. We have had an imperial government, but no imperial tax. An imperial system of defense—which makes Europe and Japan American military protectorates—has coexisted with an increasingly plural economic system. A powerful European bloc, while depending upon American troops and missiles for military security, resists American hegemony in trade and money. Hence, an integrated trans-Atlantic monetary system has never been able to find a stable equilibrium. In other words, the postwar monetary disorder, like that of the interwar period, stems ultimately from the lack of consensus about the basic political-economic relationships among the developed capitalist states.

In addition to this long-standing failure to achieve a viable trans-Atlantic political-economic equilibrium, the contemporary malaise in the capitalist world increasingly reflects a widespread belief that the era of rapid growth is drawing to a close. Throughout the postwar era, incipient domestic and international conflicts among the developed states have been smoothed by a steadily rising standard of living. That rise now appears threatened. Food and other raw materials seem increasingly scarce in relation to the demands of a growing world population. Faith in technology has been shaken by a new awareness of the spiraling environmental and social costs of industrial growth.

Views about the nature and significance of a new scarcity, of course, vary widely. Some believe the recent shortages are essentially artificial—political rather than economic. Oil is scarce, it is said, because of the producers' cartel rather than because of any natural scarcity. What is created by political means may be destroyed by the same means.[5] Others believe the market will itself restore a cheap and abundant oil supply, which can be translated to mean that the producers lack sufficient political consensus to sustain their cartel in the face of an inevitable decline in demand. Both views anticipate, in effect, a restoration of the imperial system. Power, they believe, remains unequal; so therefore will economic welfare among states also remain unequal. For many, moreover, technology remains a bright hope to sustain growth in the future. Some regard the concern with pollution a luxurious fad, fated to pass in a more serious world. Some believe population control can eventually stabilize world demand at manageable levels. Optimists look to the vast riches of the seabeds or unlimited energy from nuclear fusion. But such optimism about continuing growth, if not dead, is inhibited and doubtful. Any attempt to imagine a stable new world system can hardly ignore the reassessment of growth, a subject to which I would like to return later.

In any event, the present political-economic situation is difficult enough even without the prospect of a long-range economic decline. These immediate contradictions have prevented a stable political economic equilibrium, even within the Pan-Atlantic system.

Immediate Prospects: a New Economic Nationalism

Prolonged disequilibrium, in the 1960s as in the 1920s, has gradually fragmented the international liberal order. It remains to be seen whether a crash and prolonged depression will accompany this fragmentation. The progress of economic sophistication has widely been assumed to preclude such extremities, but confidence now wanes significantly. At the very least, as states seek to reestablish a domestic equilibrium shaken by participation in a disordered international system, a movement toward protectionism seems inevitable. The simultaneous disintegration of the Far Empire, and the consequent fear of raw-materials shortages, further encourages economic nationalism and blocs. Industrial countries will naturally seek special bilateral or group relations with their suppliers. In short, economic nationalism seems a likely response to America's disintegrating imperial order. Each major economic unit will seek to shelter itself and will carefully regulate and negotiate its participation in the international system.[6]

This general analysis suggests two major and closely related questions about the future:

1. What is the likely scope of the economic units in the coming period of economic nationalism? Will the "blocs" be national or regional? In particular, will the European Community survive?
2. What are the alternatives for ultimately reconstituting a new international system?

It may be easier to examine the second question first.

Reconstituting the International Economic Order: Models for the Future

Whatever its form, we can hope the coming period of nationalist withdrawal will be followed, after a period of consolidation, by a serious attempt to return to a more integrated international order. But what will be the nature of that order? Our discussion below focuses primarily on the international monetary system, although the world's political-economic system obviously has many other dimensions. The analysis concentrates on the monetary question because it is perhaps the best way to approach the larger issues; monetary systems, for all their technical aspects, are essentially a sort of metaphor for general political-economic relations in the world system. Moreover, in a world where war no longer seems feasible, the monetary system has more than ever become the arena within which states struggle to adjust their conflicting aims. And, resolving the monetary questions will also involve an overall adjustment of domestic and foreign economic relations. Any coherent settlement is bound to encompass trade, investment, aid, military burden sharing, inflation, and all the other political-economic issues. What, then, are the alternatives for a new international monetary order, itself the metaphor for the international system as a whole?

Logic, as well as historical experience, suggest two kinds of integrated monetary systems: hegemonic and plural. In an integrated system currencies are easily exchangeable. An integrated system which is hegemonic gives one country the official right to issue a reserve currency for the system as a whole, as with the Dollar Exchange Standard after the Second World War.[7] Thus, one country is exempt from the need to remain in equilibrium. By contrast, an integrated system which is plural organizes itself around rules and practices which all major centers are expected to follow, as, in theory, with the Bretton Woods system or the gold standard from 1870 to 1914. All countries were supposed to submit to an adjustment process designed to correct payments deficits and surpluses.

Hegemonic Systems

A hegemonic system resolves the crucial question of how much international money is to be created by settling the power to create it upon one country. As Mr. Cleveland has argued, hegemonic systems generally suffer from inflation. Inflation follows when the hegemonic power is unable to resist running excessive deficits in order to bolster its political, military, or economic position. Hence, as Professor Triffin pointed out in the early sixties, hegemonies tend toward technical collapse. Neither weakness is, of course, necessary. Presumably, a hegemonic system could achieve equilibrium. Such would seem to have been the condition of Britain's imperial system before World War I. Britain's large trade deficit, as well as her foreign lending and investment, were balanced by the income from the services she provided the system as a whole, including the service of governing India, and a large return on previous investments.[9]

The conditions for equilibrium within the British imperial system suggest why hegemony is unsuited to relations among equally developed industrial powers. Such powers do not easily lend themselves to a complementary division of labor, with food and raw material producers on one side and manufacturers, traders, and bankers on the other. Indeed, the British system itself eventually lost its cohesion because the dominions were no longer content to remain undeveloped industrially. As for a continuing American hegemony in the postwar era, it is difficult to imagine the Europeans acquiesing in a permanent industrial inferiority to the United States. America's political deficit, for troops and investments abroad, is unlikely to be made up either by a huge American trade surplus, which would seriously harm European efforts to maintain advanced industrial technology, or by a vastly increased American income from international services, which would rob Europeans of a large part of their traditional roles as bankers and traders. A declining and disunited Europe, of, course, may feel compelled to acquiesce in such a relationship with the United States. Such an arrangement is unlikely, however, to remain stable, particularly in the face of shrinking world resources. More radical European governments could be expected, in due course, to take more drastic action to disengage. In other words, a resurgence of American hegemony, and the dollar standard, is likely to provoke a renewal of monetary disintegration. Such a system is never likely to reach a stable equilibrium.

Perhaps such a view is unnecessarily gloomy. Why, it might be asked, would the United States be incapable of disciplining itself to remain in balance, or to create just enough international liquidity, by its deficits, to finance the steady growth of world trade and investment? The answer springs more from politics than economics. It is the answer which those who prefer a balance of power have always proposed to those who prefer an imperial order: Power corrupts. It is unlikely that monetary hegemony will not eventually be abused. Abuse seems particularly unavoidable when the hegemon is the most powerful of the world's nation-states, with a domestic economy highly self-sufficient and thus relatively invulnerable to the consequences of a world economic breakdown. Unless contained within an effectively organized structure of constraint, the temptation for the United States to overextend, or to resolve its domestic difficulties at the expense of the world at large, must prove nearly inevitable.

Plural Systems

The inevitable corruption of any national hegemon, plus the inevitable resistance of the other powers, form, of course, the principal rationale for a plural rather than a hegemonic system. Plural integrated systems may be divided into two broad categories: multilaterally managed and automatic. A multilaterally managed system tries, in effect, to combine plural equality with centralized control. A central authority manages the system on the basis of a negotiated political consensus among the partners. The conference at Bretton Woods was to have created such an arrangement. This, in theory, has also the organizing principle of organizations like the GATT, the OECD, the Groups of Ten and then Twenty, NATO, and even the UN Security Council. In practice, these organizations reveal the essential weakness of a multilateral structure. Insofar as the organization is truly multilateral, the partners will have great difficulty in reaching agreement on significant issues. Multilateral organizations are thus either a cover for the hegemony of one power, as with NATO, or else have little real coordinating power, as with the IMF, the GATT and the OECD. The difficulty arises less from the stupidity or weakness of states than from the inherent difficulty of negotiating policies which reconcile the interests of so many different national systems—each with its own special environment and set of forces.

The problem, moreover, is not easily resolved by transferring the burden from national delegates to a supranational staff of technical experts. While ingenious expertise can often do much to eliminate needless friction, genuine conflicts of national and group interests are unlikely to disappear. When the decision of a supranational body conflicts with the strong national interest of important partners, they will resist and, if necessary, disengage from the system. International bureaucrats, gifted with normal instincts for survival, will retreat from such confrontations. Those who do not will find themselves deserted.[10] Such are the realities of our plural world of nation-states, a world in which political divisions only reflect the wide diversity of mankind's cultural and economic environment.

Thus international institutions which are truly multilateral tend to flourish either when they deal with highly technical matters which can safely be left to experts, or else are limited to members who share a common situation and interest. But economic issues, and particularly monetary issues, are highly political and have grown increasingly so throughout this century. Significantly, the most successful of the world's multilateral organizations has been the European Communities. The states of Europe, without giving up their sovereignty, have nevertheless been able to coordinate policies sufficiently to obtain a high degree of economic integration. Obviously their multilateral confederation is aided by the great similarity of their political-economic systems, their present advantageous economic interdependence, their shared experiences in the past, and their growing sense of a shared fate for the future. Nevertheless, the difficulties of consolidating their economic union remain very great—despite their current high degree of integration and impressive experience with joint economic management. The difficulties, therefore, of an even more extended economic union, such as proposals for a monetary system organized around the IMF imply, seem formidable.

Automatic Plural Systems. A second form of plural integrated system remains to be considered, namely an automatic system organized around certain accepted rules of the game. Such was the character, at least in theory, of the gold standard before the First World War. In practice, such a monetary system does not preclude discretionary management to smooth out temporary imbalances or soften the effects of adjustment. But it does impose the obligation to maintain convertibility and not to use governmental controls and interventions to cancel the adjustment process.

While an automatic system thus does not preclude economic management at both the national and international levels, it suggests to many analysts a greater degree of international liberalism than seems compatible with a commitment to full employment—the political policy of most advanced nations and essential, many believe, to continuing economic, social, and political stability. To argue this is perhaps to admit that most countries cannot retain domestic social and political equilibrium without a higher degree of inflation than a system of prompt automatic adjustment would allow. Of course, if all nations inflate equally, or if an ample supply of increasing international liquidity is properly distributed throughout the system, then prompt adjustments can be reconciled with growth as well as with inflation. Such a necessary increase in liquidity could, in theory, be achieved by providing more Special Drawing Rights or by periodically revaluing the price of gold itself. But all nations are not equally tolerant of inflation. And solving the question of the amount and distribution of new liquidity confronts the basic problem of any multilateral system for reconciling a great variety of national environments and perspectives.

Jacques Rueff and the Gold Standard. The gold standard before 1914 is the major historical illustration claimed by advocates of a plural automatic system. The most distinguished and interesting advocate of a return to the gold standard has long been Jacques Rueff.[11] Rueff combines an impressive technical mastery and broad historical and philosophical perspective with an engaging modesty and common sense. His ideas, however, have never been taken seriously by Anglo-Saxon economists, for reasons, one suspects, which do them little credit. Fundamentally, Rueff's views reflect a greater concern with stability than with growth, a perspective out of fashion in the postwar boom. For Rueff, inflation is the great disease of modern society—the easy way to appease man's unlimited greed exacerbated by the wiles of a commercialized society. But inflation, Rueff believes, becomes habit forming for the society that adopts it. And the inflationary habit leads not only to a dangerous restlessness among all classes, those who are benefited and those who suffer, but to a decline in saving and hence in investment and real growth. Rueff's views have seemed out of touch with an era which has looked to limitless growth, stimulated by government, to resolve fundamental social and political problems. With growth, as Max Weber long ago observed, the poor can get richer without the rich becoming poorer. For a bourgeois society which hopes to remain plural, growth has seemed the easy alternative to Marxist revolution. Rueff, of course, is hardly a Marxist. Instead, he is a good French bourgeois searching for a prosperous but ordered society, with political and economic liberty for individuals and whose hierarchies are open to talent and are mitigated by national fraternity. Rueff shares little of the spirit of Keynes' Bloomsbury; original sin remains an operating concept in this thought. Unlike many latter-day Keynesians, he does not believe a little inflation the best way to save bourgeois society.

Rueff's views on the monetary system illustrate, among other things, the tendency among many conservatives to look to an international system to reinforce domestic discipline. In a common version of this phenomenon, many of Europe's rich support a continuing American hegemony as a bulwark against any drastic domestic experiments. In Rueff's belief, however, American monetary hegemony has imported a foreign disease into French society. But nationalist isolationism from a contaminating world is not his cure. Quite the contrary, autarchy, he fears, would only tempt the state to extend further its

control over the society, a development which will, he believes, strain economic efficiency, weaken individual liberties
and increase the tendency to replace the market by politics.
The temptation to state socialism would be all the more
compelling in a society suddenly deprived of the drug of inflationary growth. Autarchy, then, is no solution. A sound
national system, in Rueff's view, cannot be built in isolation; a
sound national system and a sound international system are
interdependent. His is a perspective, of course, particularly
appealing to those who fear the decline of industrial discipline and the thrusting demand for higher profits and wages.

Rueff's unfashionable views may enjoy an unexpected re-
vival. Not only, of course, will his predictions of international
monetary collapse seem to have been confirmed by events, but
the spreading indignation about inflation is likely to make him
more acceptable. In the longer term, the new awareness of the
limits and costs of growth, and the consequent domestic and
international dangers of its waning, should reinforce Rueff's
conservative emphasis on equilibrium through objective rules.
If modern societies are to be deprived of easy growth, an
embattled bourgeoisie may increasingly find Rueff's classic
perspective the best safeguard and justification for its own
survival, as well as that of liberal society in general. In other
countries, as in France herself, however, a shift to Rueffian
perspectives is unlikely actually to end the interventionist role
of the state and restore laissez-faire. Neither the welfare state
nor neomercantilism are likely to recede. Rather, the restoration of more classic perspectives may qualify the fashionable
inclination to see economic resources and reactions as infi-
nitely malleable to political power. The classic virtues of self-
restraint, thrift, patience, and resignation—so essential to a
free bourgeois society—may regain prestige as the Rueffian
view of the natural order seems increasingly relevant to a real
world of scarcity. In de Gaulle's language, certain "cold rules of
reason," needed to discipline even the most ardent genius,
may regain their former prestige.

To predict a new respect for equilibrium is not, of course, to expect a return to the laissez-faire of the classical gold standard. Can we speak of a neomercantilist gold standard? Even in the pre-1914 era, it seems, governments and central banks played a large managing role in monetary matters.[12] The "rule" of the gold standard was not that governments and central banks must passively accept equilibrating gold movements, but rather that the major centers must, through a combination of policy and market forces, remain in rough equilibrium with each other. Movements of gold were perhaps not so much themselves the means of adjustment as the signals of disequilibrium which triggered monetary authorities into corrective action. Such a mercantilist view of the historic gold standard makes it a good deal more relevant to the present world than the traditional laissez-faire model. Modern states will naturally seek to retain mercantilist control over their national economic environments and regulate participation in the international system so as to screen out disruptive external forces. Nevertheless, even if our world is inevitably mercantilist, a new respect for the advantages of rules which encourage mutual restraint and good faith would help temper the Faustian belief that all is possible for those whose will is endowed with power. An updated gold standard could reinforce that restraint.

These ruminations have an analog in the international sphere where, since the war, the United States has exulted in its new power and sense of mission. If the United States does finally cure itself of its imperial virus, and return to a more restrained view of its own capabilities, as well as a greater respect for the interest and power of other states, a Rueffian view of measure may seem a more appropriate guide to organizing the international system. Respect for equilibrium at home and abroad will be mutually reinforcing. Once such a consensus was reached among the major capitalist states, an updated gold standard might provide the system of rules to govern their monetary relations. Such a balanced monetary regime is, of course, suited to an overall international system that is plural rather than hegemonic.

Floating. The current version of an automatic system, however, is not the Rueffian gold standard but floating. Floating might not be thought an integrated system at all, but rather the necessary consequence of a breakdown in integration. In a widespread view, however, floating is thought to combine the advantages of international economic integration with national monetary independence. Floating, it is believed, will permit states to conduct whatever domestic policy seems most appropriate. The differing rates of money growth in each country will be reflected in changing exchange rates. Adjustment will eventually take place in trade, but without capital controls or unwelcome restraints on domestic economic policies.

For the reasons spelled out by Hans Schmitt among others, the floating system has not worked as anticipated, nor is it likely to do so. Floating will remain dirty, that is to say, managed, because states are unwilling to leave their exchange rates, upon which their exports and often their advanced technology depends, to a market whose decisions are likely to seem rigged, capricious, or anyway unfavorable.[13] Moreover, it is impractical to ignore the distinction between commercial and political outflow. A dollar depreciation to restore an American trade balance may be acceptable. But a depreciation to produce a trade surplus to pay for America's military and investment outflows will very likely meet foreign resistance.

In effect, floating has simply become a technical means for negotiating exchange rates among the major monetary powers within that nationalist or bloc system which has gradually been replacing the postwar dollar standard. Thus floating is not so much a system as a reflection of that unresolved conflict between hegemony and pluralism which still prevents an integrated system.

How are the models from our catalog of systems likely to display themselves in the latter part of this century?

Prospects for the Future

With a continuing disequilibrium, a continuing deterioration of international economic relations seems inevitable. No doubt, our capacity to manage crises, economic and political, has seemed to grow greatly in recent years. Nevertheless, the once prevailing confidence that any situation can be handled has begun to be undermined by the suspicion that our skills in postponement may, in the end, have been bought at the price of timely reform. The ultimate breakdown might prove all the more catastrophic. And effects of such a major breakdown upon domestic economies and social-political systems might well lead to authoritarian regimes ill-disposed to international cooperation. Such, after all, was the pattern of the thirties. While another trans-Atlantic war seems unthinkable in the nuclear age, it remains to be seen whether capitalist states will have found alternative ways to restore their economic systems or to rejuvenate their national unity. If not, our Western societies may come to see those sharp and unwelcome domestic mutations which have convulsed many other parts of the world.

There are, of course, happier alternatives. There remains the hope of the Atlanticists that, after a period of disintegration and menacing chaos, a chastened Europe and Japan will return to the comforts of American hegemony. A truly international order may then follow, based upon a benevolent American imperium suitably modified by multilateral institutions for consultation. Those who think this way may be right. I myself fear that, as in the interwar period, a lingering pretension to hegemony will frustrate serious reform until the time for easy remedies is past. Europe and America, like France and Britain between the wars, will defeat each other, to their mutual cost.

In such an event, the Europeans should perhaps be blamed

more than the Americans. Human nature being what it is, no state can be expected to resist indefinitely temptations to hegemony and exploitation over weak, divided, and rich neighbors. The United States has already demonstrated a rather singular virtue in this respect. It tempts fate to expect such virtue to continue in an increasingly straitened world economy.

The most promising hope, in my view, lies not in the restoration of imperial hegemony, but in the gradual evolution toward an integrated plural system. As I have been suggesting, for the short run we can doubtless expect a period of increasing controls over money and trade, while national and regional systems seek to regain their own equilibria. Subsequently, however, we may hope to see these blocs return to a more integrated and less managed relationship.

But some such new system, based upon general international equilibrium, seems more likely if the Europeans ultimately prove able to construct a functioning monetary union. A European bloc would find it easier to prevent the United States from flooding the world with excess liquidity. A European currency bloc, of course, could not be sustained without a high degree of general political cooperation among the participating states. The evolution toward such European cohesion would also work to eliminate that asymmetry between Europe's economic and military roles which has contributed so heavily to America's monetary disequilibrium. For any European coalition strong enough for a monetary bloc to be formed would also be likely to have extended itself to the security field, and be more independent militarily. A world system of American, European, and perhaps Japanese blocs could protect domestic societies from excessive external disruption, while encouraging, through a balance of power and invulnerability, a mutual renunciation of hegemonic pretensions. Such a world, should it come into existence, would possess the essential political-economic elements needed for an international monetary order based on equilibrium. A balance-of-payments equilibrium among the major centers could be sustained by a mixture of floating and controls. Perhaps, as the blocs reached a certain degree of parity in their economic strength, and as all societies, confronted by a secular slowing down in growth, searched for external reinforcements to internal discipline, our modernized, neomercantilist version of the gold standard might come to prevail. The need for steadily increasing liquidity would not then seem so urgent. In any event, liquidity needs might also be negotiated among the major blocs through whatever intergovernmental mechanism they might evolve. Such a monetary system would mean, in effect, that the major centers had adjusted themselves to living in a plural world. For, as I argued at the outset, a plural monetary system would also mean a plural world political-economic system, with interdependence regulated by a shared consensus among self-determining subsystems.

Much, therefore, would seem to depend upon whether the major European powers can sustain their economic community. If they do, the bloc system will be regional; a European bloc will exist along side a dollar bloc, and perhaps a Japanese bloc. Two or three strong political-economic systems, each capable of sustaining internal equilibrium and prosperity as well as demanding nonhegemonic external relations, can perhaps bring the present chaos to an end and negotiate a stable and relatively open international system.

An integrated Europe balancing the United States within an interdependent Atlantic system is scarcely a novel blueprint for the evolution of the postwar system. While the mutual advantages of such a structure are perhaps theoretically obvious, achieving closely integrated policies among the European states remains a formidable task. Moreover, while the United States might ultimately benefit greatly from a stable and more independent Europe, American resistance is only to be expected. Numerous interests on both sides of the Atlantic have a stake in continuing American hegemony and the disequilibrium which accompanies it. American corporations and banks have been greatly assisted in their foreign investments by the dollar's role. Even if an end to monetary hegemony might ultimately benefit their interests, they are likely to resist it. An end to monetary hegemony is also likely to mean either a sharp reduction in American military spending abroad, or else a significantly greater contribution from Europe and Japan for their American protection. Not even France has yet shown enthusiasm for this development, even if a more independent European defense grows more interesting and feasible.

Finally, a European bloc requires sustaining or financing a balance among Europe's states as well as a collective balance with the world outside. Sustaining an internal European equilibrium is thought to require a close harmonization of national economic policies, with perhaps a high degree of collective management over the money supply in each country. Obviously, the money supply is a vital lever for the political control of national economic life. European states have their own styles of monetary management, designed to serve their particular economic position and social and political structure. In a bloc, states in a strong exchange position, like Germany, may well have to carry states in a weak position, like Italy. For weak states, like Italy or England, fidelity to a bloc may not only rob them of flexibility in dealing with their problems, but place them under domination by their stronger partners. Hence, common monetary policies, or even rules, are difficult to negotiate, and the task is not likely to be turned over to some technical authority. With such obstacles, Europe's slow progress toward monetary union is hardly surprising. Certainly no supranational managing structure seems likely for any foreseeable future. Does this mean an effective European bloc is impossible?

Much current analysis assumes that a bloc must be hegemonic to survive. One power or some federal structure is supposed to dominate. This view merely extends to the European confederacy the British imperial view of the international system or the American federal view of our domestic system. With such a predisposition, the Anglo-American political imagination is handicapped in grasping hold of today's Europe. Europe's confederal structure manifestly fails to deprive states of their national sovereignty, but, nevertheless, reminds them of their interdependence and encourages them to seek common solutions. The confederacy may prove more effective than seems possible to the American imagination, fixed as it is upon the virtues of supranationalism. To succeed, of course, a plural confederation requires its member governments to share common perspectives and an increasing consciousness of interdependence. States cooperate reluctantly and only when pressed. Europe tends to move to union in response to crisis. Now that monetary disorder and the complications of American-Soviet rivalry in the Middle East have made prosperity precarious, Europe's governments may be inclined toward greater cohesion.

A nonhegemonic bloc also requires a certain degree of mutual strength among its members. Otherwise, the confederacy either becomes an imperial system, under a hegemonic power, or it breaks up. Members must thus be at a roughly comparable stage of economic development and must feel sufficiently strong to compete with each other without relying on the usual protectionist crutches or outside allies. In short, for the European bloc to survive and become a pillar in a new world system, an economic and political equilibrium must exist among its principal members, each of whom must be in a reasonable state of economic and political health. Hence, the disappointing truth that countries like England and Italy cannot solve their internal difficulties by joining the Common Market. On the contrary, to participate successfully in a European confederation, they must control successfully their domestic economic and political weaknesses.

Whether the various European states can achieve such an internal and collective equilibrium obviously remains a matter of conjecture. The difficulties are clear enough. However, in a world of apparently shrinking resources, so too are the costs of continuing disunity. As de Gaulle once argued so eloquently, an interdependent system, to function properly, demands that its members cultivate the strength and the will to uphold their own interests. Otherwise, they do not make their own indispensable contribution to equilibrium within a system. And, as de Gaulle certainly believed, they deserve what they get. Sooner or later the European states will have to face up to their world responsibilities, or expect to pay the price of weakness.

Other Dimensions of the World System

East-West. Our analysis of the world political economy has been preoccupied with relations among the advanced capitalist countries, essentially between Europe and the United States. What of the communist systems of Russia and China, or the developing economies of the the Third or Fourth World? Each is a vast subject in itself. A few paragraphs may at least suggest their relation to our general analysis.

Postwar international studies have focused heavily on relations between the United States and the Soviet Union, particularly military relations. Little by little, however, the Cold War, and the general preoccupation with the communist world, will be seen as a diversionary interlude in modern world history. The Cold War vision, two superpowers competing to organize the globe, appears increasingly theatrical and implausible. Only the temporary weakness of the other power centers permitted the superpowers these inflated pretensions. And it is their ambitions to organize the globe, rather than anything fundamental in their mutual situations, which have led to conflict between Russia and America. Essentially, neither Russia nor America has much to do with the other, nor will they. Only when each imagines itself dominating the world do they come into contact. Detente, based on mutual indifference, is their normal relation. In short, interdependence, not isolation, breeds conflict. The United States has fought two world wars with Europe, not with the Soviet Union.

The Russians, it may be said, recognized their limitations rather earlier than we. Indeed, the revisionist view of postwar history strongly suggests that Stalin, from the first, resolutely concentrated on consolidating Russia's national position, and firmly rejected the seductions of even European hegemony. The Russians, having so often endured Europe's exuberance, have perhaps acquired a more mature sense of the danger of overextension than have the Americans.

If Russia and America have only tangential relations, Russia nevertheless is of an immediate concern for Europe. Russia and communism are indeed a threat, but only in the same sense that bacteria are a threat to human beings. A body politic weakened from its own internal imbalance can succumb to disease. If Western liberal societies fail to solve their problems, they will doubtless sink into some form of authoritarian domestic political system—either of the left or the right. And if Western European states cannot achieve some minimal degree of cohesion among themselves, they are open to the domination of powerful outsiders. De Gaulle's hope that superpower rivalry would allow European powers great room for maneuver has proved to be illusory, essentially because that superpower rivalry is itself illusory. History now gives the European states few options for independence other than their own cohesion.

What of the economic role of Russia? While trade between Russia and the West will doubtless increase, the Soviet system will never open itself to become closely integrated with an international system which it cannot hope to control. The Russians know they cannot control Western Europe. Russia will thus remain essentially autarchic, the mercantilist state par excellence.

Are the Eastern European states tied to Russia's autarchic future? It is difficult to say. Perhaps the Russians, relying on ideological predilection, military force, and economic blandishment, can succeed in holding the Eastern European economies within a Soviet bloc. But the contrary pull of the Western economies will remain strong and is likely to increase. The Eastern European situation has, therefore, the makings of real conflict—not between America and Russia but between Russia and Western Europe. Still, Eastern Europe is no longer a vital interest for the Western European states. The realities of nuclear weapons suggest that no one is likely to force a Russian devolution from the outside. Old hopes for Russian devolution, of course, remain. Eastern Europe and Russia herself may liberalize. A Russia, locked in conflict with China over her vast Asian colonies, may seek a genuine European settlement. But these advanced hopes lack conviction in the face of Russia's millennial tenacity, despotism, and strength.

In short, the Soviet system is likely to remain a world apart—its relations with the capitalist powers carefully regulated to preserve Russia's own national interests. Interdependence will not be allowed to grow until it threatens stability. As this reality grows more obvious, the fundamental incentive and justification for American hegemony over Europe will disappear. The Cold War will no longer smother the inherent conflict between American hegemony and European self-determination, nor, we can hope, prevent that readjustment of relations needed to resolve it.

What may be said of Russia's autarchy obviously applies even more to China's. The Chinese, having finally driven out the foreign devils, are unlikely to invite them back wholesale. Any economic intercourse with the capitalist world will be closely regulated. As a result, once we give up our pretensions to being an Asian power, American relations with China are likely to be tranquil.

Japan, however, has special difficulties. Since the war, Japan has lived in a sort of fool's paradise. The Japanese, having failed in World War II to establish their own imperial system, received from their American conquerers all the economic benefits of empire, plus a good deal more. Not only were the Japanese given free access to raw materials, but the American market itself was thrown open to them, and without any serious reciprocity. In addition, the United States has been Japan's effective military protector. Not surprisingly, Japanese governments have found the postwar arrangements highly satisfactory. In a more straitened world, however, Japan's old problems have begun to reappear. The European market has never been opened very wide; the American market grows more restricted. Currency revaluations—part of America's own mercantilist drive—threaten Japanese competitiveness in the developed markets. Yet these are the markets, and not those of Asia or Latin America, for which postwar Japan's highly sophisticated products are largely aimed. Above all, the threatened restriction of raw materials greatly imperils Japan's political-economic structure. More than any other major power, Japan depends on a well-functioning world political economy.

Japan's likely response to her new situation lies in diversifying her political-economic connections. Most probably, she will turn her attentions more and more to the developing world, but hope to avoid any specific imperial commitments or vulnerabilities. Close military ties with the United States will be preserved as long as they seem reliable and not too expensive. Ultimately, Japan will have once more to become a military power, able at least to defend her own homeland. But the realities of the new Asia foreclose a return to her old solutions, if not her old problems. In any event, the American attempt to integrate Japan into a Pan-Atlantic economy will enjoy only a limited success.

North-South. What, finally, is to be said of the Third World, that Far Empire which has been the other half of the postwar American system? Obviously, the Third World is a teeming diversity and every part has its own problems and prospects. The United States, as befits the world imperial power, still struggles to keep the Third World integrated within a world system. Global problems, we say, require global solutions. International corporations, we argue, are the vanguard of development. While not denying the practical wisdom of much that we say, our general strategy seems destined for defeat. The nineteenth century is over, and nationalism has spread beyond Europe to Asia, Latin America, and Africa. The old imperial pattern of small nation-states, penetrated by foreign economic interests, is disappearing, unlikely to be replaced by a return to a more direct imperialism. Gradually, we can expect the more serious civilizations of the non-Western world to reassert control over their own political-economic environments. The major Asian powers are well on their way. The Middle East is evidently eager to follow.

These great transformations will not take place everywhere in one or two generations. Still, the process seems sufficiently advanced in enough places to suggest the manifest irrelevance of the hegemonic vision of world order. We have perhaps been fortunate to have had the Vietnamese experience as a preview of the nationalist world of the future. Nothing but ruin lies ahead if we cannot learn to limit our pretensions and our vulnerabilities to suit a plural world. We must begin that adjustment within the West itself. The cost of failure in the West, should we fail, will be very high. In view of the many trials coming for the world as a whole, no greater historical tragedy can be imagined than the mutual ruination of Europe and America.

Notes

[1] See C. Fred Bergsten, "The Threat From the Third World," *Foreign Policy*, No. 11 (Summer 1973).

[2] The point is developed at length in my "European Coalition in a Fragmenting World," *Foreign Affairs*, Vol. 54, No. 1 (October 1975).

3 Nearly every year since 1950, the U.S. basic balance of payments (current account plus long-term capital flows) has been negative, despite a regular trade surplus and a large and steadily growing repatriated income from U.S. foreign investments. Large negative items have been foreign military expenditures, foreign aid, and government expenditures generally, along with net flows of investment capital in the private sector. Hence the view that the U.S.deficit has been "political." By way of example, in 1970, the U.S. basic balance was $−3.0 billion: Merchandise surplus was $ + 2.2 billion and investment income was $ + 6.4 billion. Net government outflow was around $7.0 billion.

4 For the significance of a trade surplus, see Hans O. Schmitt, "International Monetary System: Three Options for Reform," *International Affairs*, Vol. 50, No. 2 (April 1974), pp. 199-205. Also H. van B. Cleveland and W. H. Bruce Brittain, "A World Depression?" *Foreign Affairs* (January 1975), pp. 235-38.

5 See, for example, my colleague Robert W. Tucker, "Oil: The Issue of American Intervention," *Commentary* (January 1975).

6 For an extended discussion of why contemporary states regulate their participation in the international system, see D. P. Calleo and B. M. Rowland, *America and the World Political Economy* (Bloomington: Indiana University Press, 1973), Ch. 10.

7 Sterling was, of course, the other reserve currency in the postwar period. Its position was the legacy of Britain's former imperial role. Its fate became ever more closely tied to that of the dollar.

8 See Harold van B. Cleveland's article, *op. cit.*, and Robert Triffin, *Gold and the Dollar Crisis: The Future of Convertibility* (New Haven: Yale University Press, 1960).

9 A. R. Cairncross demonstrates that between 1870 and 1913 interest on foreign investment for Britain almost always exceeded the net export of capital. *Home and Foreign Investment, 1870-1913: Capital Accumulation* (Cambridge: Cambridge University Press, 1953). For India's contribution, see E. J. Hobsbawm, *Industry and Empire: The Making of Modern English Society* (New York: Random House, 1968), p. 305.

10 For a succinct presentation, see J. S. Nye, "Comparing Common Markets: A Revised Neo-Functionalist Mode," in *Regional Integration: Theory and Research*, ed. Leon N. Lindberg and Stuart A. Scheingold (Cambridge, Mass.: Havard University Press, 1971).

For my extended views, see my "American Foreign Policy and American European Studies: An Imperial Bias," in *The United States and Western Europe*, ed. Wolfram F. Hanrieder (Cambridge: Winthrop, 1974), pp. 73-78.

[11] Perhaps Jacques Rueff's most complete and technical exposition of his monetary theory in English is his *Balance of Payments* (New York: Macmillan, 1967). See also his more polemical *The Monetary Sin of the West* (New York: Macmillan, 1971).

[12] For a broad discussion of the prewar and interwar monetary systems, from several perspectives, see the forthcoming volume of essays sponsored by the Lehrman Institute and edited by Benjamin M. Rowland, *Balance of Power or Hegemony: The Interwar Monetary System* (New York: New York University Press, 1976).

[13] See note 4, above.

THE CREATION
OF INTERNATIONAL
MONETARY ORDER

Lewis E. Lehrman

Introduction

Today, national economic policy making is largely concerned with the problems of unemployment and inflation. More precisely, it is their simultaneous combination in nearly all Western economies which preoccupies policy makers. As these problems grow worse, the stakes rise higher. We know that either severe unemployment or sustained inflation, let alone both together, can be expected to have the most serious consequences for liberal democracy.

During the postwar era, some had imagined the issue of widespread unemployment resolved by Lord Keynes who, forty years ago in the midst of a world depression, prescribed activist fiscal and monetary policies: "It may be possible," he wrote in *The General Theory*, "by a right analysis of the problem [of unemployment], to cure the disease whilst preserving efficiency and freedom." [1] Surely it is a proper and compassionate national goal to try to eliminate large-scale unemployment if it develops during the declining phase of the business cycle. But whether ever active monetary and fiscal full-employment policies, during *all* phases of the business cycle, are compatible with a reasonable degree of economic stability, let alone efficiency and freedom, has become a major question for our times. In fact, recurring interventionist government economic policies, in themselves, appear to be unmistakable causes of the intensifying disorders which increasingly characterize the age.

Until recently, at least, the principal ailment of postwar Western economies has not been unemployment, but inflation. Indeed, if the postwar era in the liberal democracies can be accurately described as the age of Keynes, it is also the age of inflation. Inflation plagues all Western economies, even now in the midst of recession and unemployment. Everywhere the value of money deteriorates. The burden of debt, public and private, mounts ever higher. Money it seems, serves less well as a reliable store of value and the means of payment. In a worldwide exchange economy, money no longer impartially mediates between limited resources and rising expectations. Instead, political power, either of governments or of private corporations and trade unions, more and more shapes and supplants the market economy. Some Western nations thus move closer to civil war.

On a larger scale, the interdependent world economic system grows steadily more precarious. The disorders of the global economy, and in particular the disequilibrium of its monetary system, are inextricably tied up with this problem of inflation. Internationally as well as nationally, power replaces the market. The unrestrained use of political power, in pursuit of particular national economic interests, exemplifies an increasing tendency both to circumvent market disciplines and to brush aside temporarily inconvenient systems' of international rules. Nowhere, of course, has this tendency toward accentuated nationalism been more obvious than in the growing disorder of the international monetary system.

I believe that the problems of world monetary disorder,

endemic inflation, cartelization of raw materials, and unemployment are, in fact, closely linked. They originate in the excessive fiscal and monetary policies of the nation-states which compose the postwar international economic system. These harmful national policies derive their support not only from partisan groups and individuals, whose political influence displaces the true national interest with narrow sectarian goals, but also from a widespread intellectual misunderstanding of the nature of the international economic system. Popular economic doctrines have exacerbated rather than checked the spread of inflation. This potent combination of greed and fallacy has made it increasingly difficult for the world economic system to achieve stability. I would like to develop this point further, first by examining the nature of stability in the world market economy, then by discussing three major schools of national policy making and their characteristic effects upon international stability, and finally by proposing a new basis for international monetary order.

Beforehand, however, it might be useful to discuss the nature of equilibrium in both national and international contexts. What are the signs of equilibrium? In politics, the absence of a revolutionary situation (or a revolutionary party) suggests that the basic preconditions of national political equilibrium have been established. National economic equilibrium might be said to exist when the national supply and demand for goods, services, and financial claims is balanced in open markets; open markets, undisturbed by hyperactive government economic policy, will clear at regular intervals. In such circumstances, the general price level will remain relatively stable in an economy tending toward fully employed resources. Global economic equilibrium might, of course, be characterized in the same fashion. But government stabilization policies, in the national context, may actually disturb equilibrium tendencies in the international economy. In particular, some demand-management policies designed to eliminate domestic unemployment may cause widespread dislocation abroad, which, in due course, may defeat stabilization policies at home as well.

The World Market Economy

What constitutes economic equilibrium depends upon who you are and where you stand. For a housewife, economic equilibrium may exist when all members of the household are housed, fed, and clothed; when her husband is working; and when a modest provision may be easily made for savings and entertainment. To a businessman, however, the housewife's concept of equilibrium might suggest, at most, partial equilibrium—especially if the market for his products were declining, if his inventories were accumulating on the shelves, and if the cash balances needed to make current payments were available only in the form of new bank loans, which would by no means be assured if his business affairs did not take a turn for the better. A market-oriented economist would probably see both of these nontechnical definitions of equilibrium as those typical of micro-economic units, which might or might not describe conditions of general economic equilibrium. After all, the economist might argue, if the markets for goods and services cleared at prevailing prices and present employment levels, what more, in an uncertain world, could any reasonable housewife or businessman desire?

Senior economic policy makers in Washington may conceive of economic equilibrium in yet another sense. They might believe that general economic equilibrium should be characterized by full employment, low long-term interest rates, and stable prices, and that if these three conditions are not met, government fiscal and monetary policy should be immediately mobilized to achieve them. It is likely that these same policy makers would have endorsed the recent Congressional resolutions which advised the Chairman of the Federal

Reserve Board to activate an expansive monetary policy to achieve full employment, despite the obvious risk of resurgent inflation.[2]

The examples given above serve merely to emphasize different economic standpoints and methods of analysis. Different standpoints are the main sources of theoretical disagreement: The general equilibrium theory of one economist is only the partial equilibrium theory of another. Among alternative viewpoints there is one which takes the world economy as the appropriate unit of economic analysis. To quote Robert Mundell, "its basic conception is a growing world economy composed of intersecting national economies. . . . The only closed economy is the world economy."[3] Such a conception suggests that the necessary, if insufficient, condition for achieving global economic order is the adoption of national policies which are consistent with the requirements of stability in the international system as a whole. Conversely, a balanced and efficient world economic order must be the basis of a stable national economy. A global viewpoint is thus necessary in order to understand both the national and the international economic disorders of our time, for they are inextricably linked. I share this view and will endeavor to illustrate its relevance and implications.

What is the nature of the global economy? As a first approximation, I borrow from Immanuel Wallerstein's description of an emergent "European world-economy" at the dawn of the modern era:

> In the late fifteenth and early sixteenth century, there came into existence what we may call a European world-economy . . . an economic but not a political entity, unlike empires, city-states, and nation-states. In fact, it precisely encompasses within its bounds (it is hard to speak of boundaries) empires, city-states, and the emerging nation-states. It is a world system, not because it encompasses the whole world, but because it is larger than any juridically-defined political unit. And it is a

"world-economy" because the basic linkage between the
parts of the system is economic. . . . I have said that a
world-economy is an invention of the modern world. Not
quite. There were world-economies before. But they
were always transformed into empires:—China, Persia,
Rome. The modern world economy might have gone in
that same direction . . . except that the techniques of
modern capitalism and the technology of modern science
. . . enabled this world-economy to thrive, produce, and
expand without the emergence of a unified political
structure.[4]

Wallerstein's point is a valid one. For better or worse, the
modern world system is, to use his phrase, an integrated capitalist world-economy. Fundamental asymmetry and tension
develop in such a world because national economies are substantially integrated into an interdependent world economic
system, while national polities are not.[5] Close to two hundred
sovereign nation-states, almost ten times the pre-World War I
number, are the constituent elements of the world political
system of our day. The rules and institutions by which to
govern such a political system are even less identifiable than
the all-too-controversial laws of economics. This fundamental
lack of complementarity between an integrated worldwide
economic system of trade and exchange, largely subject to the
rules of market economics, and an international political system of jealously independent national communities is, we may
say, the basic problem of international order. What combination of two hundred independent national economic policies
would be consistent with the requirements of a stable world
economic order? At what price to national sovereignty must
the public good of world economic stability be purchased?

To some extent there is agreement in academia, on Wall
Street, on Main Street, and abroad that a desirable world
economic order should be characterized by full employment,
stable prices, low long-term interest rates, in exchange for
which many economic nationalists might even be willing to

accept some compromise to national sovereignty. National political leaders forever debate how to get from "here to there." Despite informal international agreements on vague and general aims, statesmen will, moreover, continue to guard their economic sovereignty. They do so not merely from a love of power but from the belief that, in the real world, they need their independence to safeguard unique national interests. In practice, for better or worse, policies which affect the world market economy will continue to be decided in national political centers.

It would be disingenuous, of course, to overlook the unequal economic conditions of these national communities, or the unequal weight which various countries exert on the world economy. While the great nations of the West may perceive unequal national conditions to be understandable, even inevitable, historical developments, the energetic poor nations may be expected to read history differently. Peaceful accommodation among the unequal participants in international affairs presumably depends upon establishing those institutions and rules which encourage cooperation among contentious countries if only to mitigate unfair and destructive competition for economic advantage.

In any event, if the world economy and the national economy are as intimately related as I have argued, assessing the impact of national economic policy making requires not only a consideration of its domestic consequences but also a careful evaluation of its effects upon the world.

Three Schools of Thought

I shall briefly characterize, from this international perspective, three schools of thought which prescribe economic policies, directly or indirectly designed to effect national output, employment, and the general price level. Each school measures the relative merits of the government's monetary and fiscal policies by their contribution to national economic goals. All three schools assign a more or less prominent role to the free-market economy.

Keynesians and Monetarists

One school originated in the 1930s and its economics dominated the intellectual debates of the 1950s and 1960s. "Its premises reflect the uncertainties of that decade [the 1930s] ... assumed rigid wages, no growth, a closed [national] economy.... [It was] a short-run model ... dominated by pessimistic expectations." [6] Oversimplified, this was the basis of the Keynesian model. To a great extent this theory subordinated the goal of world economic stability, historically measured by balance-of-payments equilibrium and exchange-rate stability, to national policies designed to achieve full domestic employment. In this sense, Keynesian economic policy may be described as a contemporary nationalist version of an older mercantilist standpoint.

It has been argued by some Keynesians, moreover, that a government-shaped economy ought to displace, if only to stabilize at a higher level of activity, a less-politicized, underemployed free-market economy. To effect this displacement, Keynesians encouraged governments to mobilize a dormant national asset, hitherto utilized only in wartime situations: the fiscal franchise of the state apparatus, that is to say, the taxing and spending power of the modern nation-state. The use of this franchise in peacetime, along with an expansive monetary policy, became known as aggregate demand management, needed, it was said, to achieve full national employment. Because domestic price stability was generally a subordinate consideration, one predictable result of neo-Keynesian demand management policies has been inflation of the general price level.

In the postwar Western world, the advent of government demand management, by means of ever active national monetary and fiscal policies, has, as I note above, politicized the economic process and marked a decisive decline in the primacy of the private market economy.[7] This development, of course, has presented our political and economic systems with many new problems. As I have argued earlier, these problems have more than national implications. For reasons which I develop below, national economic disorders, which result from unforeseen excesses of the Keynesian revolution, are soon passed on to the international economy as well. Moreover, if the political process is to decide the allocation of resources and the distribution of income, how can essentially coercive political decisions be reconciled with economic liberty, economic efficiency, and fiscal discipline? How, in a free society, can a nation forestall the misappropriation of growing government economic power by organized special interests—whether they be military establishments, improvident corporations, trade unions, or sprawling welfare bureaucracies?

But we are contending today with much more than the legacy of the Keynesian revolution. There is also the now-fashionable and powerful monetarist school of thought, generally identified with the University of Chicago and with Milton Friedman. This school developed largely in opposition to neo-Keynesian orthodoxy during the 1950s and 1960s. To the extent that its theorists advocate the principle of price flexibility in a free-market economy, the monetarist school draws inspiration from the classical tradition represented by David Hume, Adam Smith, David Ricardo, and Jean-Baptiste Say. However, many monetarists (assuming that the effects of monetary policy are more neutral and efficient influences on output and resource allocation than neo-Keynesian fiscal policies) in effect elevate the state over the market by asserting the supremacy and independence of national monetary policy. In other words, as Keynesian fiscalists invoke the state's taxing and spending power to modify free-market outcomes, some monetarists similarly invoke the state's control over the money supply. Thus, to encourage the government to achieve opti-

mum employment levels in a mixed-market economy, monetarists recommend specific national monetary policies. Some
monetarists have recommended a national monetary rule of
constancy, say a 3 percent growth rate in the national money
supply. Others recommend a variable rate of growth in the
money supply. Many advoate a monetary policy designed to
maintain low interest rates. All seek to influence domestic
production, employment, and price levels and also to provide
financial reserves for a growing national economy.

To achieve these specific economic growth rates, central
bankers have often been persuaded to try to impose their
policies upon national monetary aggregates or interest rates.
An aggressive central bank, presumably in pursuit of full employment, has often implemented its policies with little regard
for price stability or the free market process of allocating credit
and determining interest rates. The predictable result of hyperactive central-banking policies, at least during the past
decade, has been the inflation of the general price level. In
short, while for each monetarist there may well be a unique
monetary policy, nevertheless, for most, monetary policy is an
instrument by which the sovereign nation-state can shape the
domestic market. Perversely, as it happens, an interventionist
monetarism often combines in national policy with an interventionist Keynesianism. The latter dogma encourages government deficits, the former finances them. The combined
doctrine, called "fine tuning," has ruled the market place of
economic ideas for a generation.

For many members of the monetarist school, moreover, the
international implications of their domestic monetary pre-
scriptions do not appear to weigh very heavily. Many do not
appear to give much thought to how world economic benefits
might be inequitably and inefficiently distributed among
unequal nation-states as a result of the United States Federal
Reserve System's pursuit of a nationalist monetary policy.
They do not perceive that the monetary policy of the United
States, designed primarily to affect the general price level

domestically and the level of unemployment nationally, could lead to the reduction or redistribution of production, employment, and income throughout the rest of the world. The fact is that the short-run objectives of national monetary policy, especially the national monetary policy of a great power, have serious global implications. The monetary policy of the United States particularly affects monetary conditions in many foreign countries because the dollar is a reserve currency and, in its role as world money, serves as the basis for other national currencies. Leaving aside for the moment the theories of optimal currency areas, reasonable men might well wonder why management responsibility for a common world currency is permitted to gravitate to a single government, the national self-interest of which may only rarely coincide with an efficient and equitable distribution of world economic benefits. To understand the significance of this point, we might pause for a moment to consider why the power to create and to regulate international money is so important to the average citizen and therefore why he should be reluctant to delegate this unique power to any foreign government. The money supply of a contemporary nation-state consists primarily of the liabilities of its central and commercial banking system. How that money supply is regulated will, of course, directly affect the value of assets denominated in that currency. An expansionary or contractionary monetary policy must inevitably benefit some and harm others.

United States citizens are, as the creditors of their government and banks, subject to the authority of their duly constituted monetary authority. Whatever United States citizens may think of the national monetary policy, it is nevertheless, the monetary policy of their own legitimate governmental authorities, in whose election they have participated and over whom their collective opinion must have some influence. But the currency area of the dollar incorporates many nations of the world. And it is quite a different matter of political obligation if one is a citizen of another country. As a holder of dollars, a foreigner objects to the debasing of the value of his asset by an extraterritorial monetary authority, the control of which may not be subject to his vote or influence. Of course, no alien need maintain his creditor position in United States dollars or bank deposits. He may liquidate them in the market if he disapproves of American monetary policy and its effect on the value of his assets. But this privilege may come as little comfort to those foreign governments which, over the years, have been persuaded, in the larger interests of the stability of the world monetary system as a whole, to accumulate their reserves in these currencies now subject to the depreciation brought about by their liquidation in the foreign-exchange market.

While it takes a willing foreign creditor to accumulate his assets in United States dollars or sterling liabilities, nevertheless, it is in the nature of an *official* reserve currency system to encourage the accumulation abroad of the reserve currency, say, sterling or dollar claims, in both private hands and in the currency reserves of foreign central banks. For reasons to be discussed below, these reserve currencies almost inevitably become overvalued. Later, under changed circumstances and often in periods of stress and bitter national conflict, the crumbling reserve-currency system cannot forestall the disorderly liquidation of these same reserve currencies. If the period of liquidation and currency depreciation is accompanied by trade wars, or tariffs, or competitive exchange-rate changes, it is little comfort to hear from the historian that such is often the outcome of a breakdown in the hegemonic currency system, bound as it must be to the strengths and weaknesses of a sovereign national monetary policy and its unique national political interests. It is even less reassuring to argue that although such an unhappy outcome characterized the period of the 1930s, it certainly does not characterize that of the 1970s, if only for the reason that the tale is not yet fully told.[8]

Classicists

In Europe, the seventeenth and eighteenth centuries were characterized by frequent wars, bankrupt dynasties, mercantilist national policies, high and proliferating taxes, and the impoverishment of productive social groups as a result of substantial and unpredictable governmental intervention in the domestic and external trade of the nation. Here was fertile ground for the development of a revolutionary doctrine of political and economic liberty which advocated the careful delimitation of the scope and competence of the government's powers. Classical liberal economic theory called for balance in the government budget, reduction of certain taxes in the long-run interest of national economic welfare, and positive law in matters of public and private contracts. According to this school of economic thought, sound money and private market sovereignty, established and maintained by strong but constitutionally limited governments, would preserve liberty and orderly growth in the world society of nations, a society which, to endure, must be characterized by balance, equity, and a sense of limitation.

Equity in such a civil society depended on the subordination of the infinite desires of governments and individual citizens to the limitations of their earned and real resources. Real resources in the classical liberal view had to be earned and thereby gave rise to the genuine financial claims of an individual, an enterprise, or a nation. Economic society was delicately held together by the fact that the claims (assets) of the creditor were the counterparts of the financial liabilities of the debtor. As these claims were often held by workers, producers, and pensioners in near-money form (such as bonds and bank deposits), money was expected to maintain a constant purchasing value. To this end society provided the necessary institutional discipline over the creation and abuse of purchasing power, that is to say, money. Should the outstanding financial liabilities of an individual or corporation exceed the assets available to reimburse them, insolvency occurred. and liquidation ensued. Men respected money, therefore. Not to do so meant financial extinction. If the goal of such a social system was equity to the useful and lawful producer, bankruptcy provided its indispensable economic discipline.

Finally, classical economic theory assumed an integrated and growing international economy, an open world market with price flexibility, and a stable supply and demand for money. The classical international monetary system tried to rule out global monetary inflation through a treaty agreement among nations to abide by the inherent limitations of the gold standard system. Nations voluntarily limited their sovereignty, that is to say, their monetary autonomy, by subscribing to a regime of fixed exchange rates based upon currency convertibility into gold. The financial discipline of gold convertibility was the simple regulating mechanism of the international economy. Interestingly, bankruptcy of the improvident firm (or individual) had a political counterpart among undisciplined nations. When the financial claims on a government exceeded its capacity to reimburse them, the result was the loss of acceptance of its currency on world markets followed by the turmoil of monetary depreciation. Sound money was therefore the basis of an ordered world economy, according to this classical view.

There was little but eternity to mitigate the severe law of limitation which the threat of bankruptcy enforced on individuals and states alike. An ordered society was not organized to satisfy men's infinite desires but rather to establish and to maintain the public interest, strictly defined among its producing members by the stable rules of economic equity. Within the framework of the market economy, sternly upheld by the state and reenforced by the essential equilibrium of the international order, private preferences would then prevail in a free and open society.

Nowadays, this view is not often seriously considered. Instead, it has become altogether too easy for some to identify the public interest with the interests of the government bureaucracy itself and with government financing of private (and often insolvent) individual and corporate interests. All sorts of self-seeking parochial interests have joined their efforts in an unholy alliance to plunder the public treasury in order to forestall the bankruptcy which would inevitably overtake them, were they required by the market to finance their demands on society with real resources. This process, by which vested interests commandeer the state to serve their narrow interests, takes many forms. Oligopolistic businesses seek subsidies under the pretexts of national welfare and military security—and even more subsidies when they feel threatened by foreign competitors. Labor unions seek and obtain restrictive government legislation to enforce their monopoly control over the price, the working conditions, the supply, and the apprenticeship of labor in order to require the community to subsidize union members' wages at a higher level than would otherwise prevail in a free and open market for the supply of labor. Government planners, bureaucrats, and legislators press to provide for the welfare of their various constituencies whose narrow interests are often tied to specific economic plans and policies which are improperly put forward as being in the national interest.

Some political authorities, moreover, are wont to congratulate themselves on the increasingly sophisticated planning techniques of today's economic management. But are these developments improvements? On the contrary, the Western world in the postwar era has been indulged, not improved, by such plans—first by the Keynesians, whose spending on behalf of special interests has run up the public debt, second by the hyperactive monetarists, whose central banking and monetary policies have financed the same debt, and finally by the socialists, whose compassionate schemes for the redistribution of income have obscured and befouled the wellsprings of national wealth and power, the true sources of which, throughout history, have been the social incentives to save and to accumulate productive capital. Though its ultimate limits are not known, the exponential growth of public and (government encouraged) private indebtedness has clearly reached an alarming level, as has the present devastating inflation which inevitably develops in a social order whose economic demands exceed the limited human and natural resources available to satisfy them.

How will the long-term national or public interest ever prevail if, in a free society, private citizens, partisan groups, and public authorities try to maximize their individual interests by seizing control of the machinery of government to advance narrow short-run goals? [9] If all tend to appropriate the public interest, who and what will insure its survival? If there are no rules to compel financial order and to insure that claims to real resources are based on work and efficiency, how can it be possible in the long run to achieve any stable, rational economic order, national or international? Clearly, some other view of the role of government and of the public interest must prevail if the national community is not to experience a permanent drive by its members toward financial disorder and insolvency. And we remember, to emphasize an earlier theme, that financial disorder in one large country spreads rapidly through the international system as a whole. Indeed, the contemporary social disease of inflation is communicated by means of an efficient, if obscure, economic mechanism which ineluctably establishes and maintains the links between national price levels throughout the global economy. We must now discuss the nature of financial linkage in order to penetrate this underlying transmission mechanism.

The Market Mechanism: Arbitrage

Some contemporary economists and historians have integrated several systemic views into a comprehensive theory of the world market economy. They have revived the classical conception of the modern world as a single integrated market economy (in which a variety of political and economic entities compete for power and prosperity). Although many of the political units in this world economy retain only the mere vestiges of the capitalist system in their domestic economies, nevertheless even they are obliged to conduct certain international economic exchanges in the framework of a world market system.[10] And to this limited extent, it may be said that even Russia and China are unmistakably a part of the closed world economy.

Over the long run, national economies tend toward international integration. The most potent economic mechanism behind this tendency is the irresistible market force of arbitrage. Entrepreneurs and agents of the state will tend to buy and sell goods (and financial assets) for a profit if price differentials exist between different segments of the market that are not fully compensated for by disparities in the costs of transportation, insurance, transactions, and information. International arbitrage, we might say, is the efficient economic mechanism whereby different national prices are equalized in world markets. It has been argued that for this mechanism to have a universal impact, the physical volume of international trade would have to be substantially larger than at present because the variety of national price disparities must be substantially greater than the number of national and international economic exchanges which tend to equalize them. The answer is that effective arbitrage tends to move the price level of a product (or a financial asset) in the United States to its higher exchange price in, say, England, with a minimum of physical movement of goods between the two places having taken place. This form of arbitrage is carried out through the spot and forward markets for goods and foreign exchange.

For example, if the spot (cash) price of copper in United States dollars drops below the equivalent spot price of copper in English pounds, net of all carrying charges, one can purchase the copper in the United States (cash) market, simultaneously sell it for the differential in the English spot market, hedge the proceeds by sale of sterling for dollars, repatriate the same, and subsequently arrange by boat to make physical delivery of the copper to England. Alternatively, one might buy copper in the spot market in the United States, and sell, for example, a three-month forward contract for the same copper in the English market, if the forward market price for copper in London reflected exactly the same spot differential. One would hedge the currency exchange risk by making a simultaneous three-month forward sale of sterling for dollars. However, instead of physically delivering the copper to England when the contract has matured, one might buy back the forward copper contract in London before its maturity, lift the hedge sale of sterling, and sell the copper in the United States cash market, if the United States price has been fully arbitraged to equality with the English market through mine and other traders' domestic purchases in the United States. In the absence of a higher, now-equalized, spot copper price in the United States, one would of course deliver the United States copper in London to fulfill the terms of the matured forward contract.

In either case, over time, one's decision to buy in the United States spot market (accompanied perhaps by other entrepreneurs) raises the United States cash copper price to the English cash price and tends to maintain it there. In the first instance one ships the goods to England, and thereby adds to the volume of international commodity trade; in the latter, one sells the copper in the United States and the physical volume of international trade in commodities does not rise. In both cases arbitrage equalizes prices in different national markets through the sensitive mechanism of international spot and forward markets for commodities and currencies. Because of universal arbitrage, price levels in different countries converge toward mutual parity over the long run, regardless of the political and administrative efforts made by national authorities to influence them otherwise. It is a mistake to assume that a minimum volume of trade between two distant countries proves their mutual economic isolation. The truth is that transnational parities in certain price relationships are achieved through interest-rate and exchange-rate changes, as well as through hedged forward-market arbitrage. Moreover, to the extent that contracts in the hedged forward markets are lifted and do not lead to actual movement of goods between nations, they tend to conceal the equilibrating effects of the arbitrage mechanism.[11] This same arbitrage mechanism transmits the inflationary consequences of expansive national monetary and fiscal policies within dominant national economies to the world at large.

Today, as in similar circumstances in the past, many economic policy makers in the United States are recommending Federal deficit spending as a means to revive national economic growth and to reduce unemployment. These goals are understandable, even if the optimum means to achieve them are debatable. Along with a compensatory fiscal policy, based on the Federal deficit, these same policy makers often advocate expansionist central bank monetary policies in the belief that an expanding money supply will finance the Federal deficit without unduly raising interest rates in the short term. It is also assumed that a larger money supply will provide the necessary financial reserves to accommodate the higher level of economic activity desired. Others believe that the monetary reserves that are created by the central bank are the indispensable means by which economic activity is accelerated to higher levels of output and employment.

The precise institutional actions required to implement these policies are very simple. The United States Federal Government experiences a cash deficit during a period of economic contraction and declining tax revenues. Instead of raising taxes or cutting expenditures, the Treasury sells bills, notes, and bonds to raise cash equal to the deficit. During the same period, the Federal Reserve buys government securities in the open market from government dealers for cash, thereby providing indirectly to the banking system the new cash resources needed to finance the Federal deficit. (The central banking authorities may also lower commercial bank reserve requirements or they may expand discounting to the commercial banking system at lower interest rates, providing even more monetary reserves to the financial markets, part of which will wind up financing the Treasury's rising demands for cash balances.) It is crucial to remember that the sole intent thus far of the economic policy makers has been to reduce domestic unemployment and to activate underutilized productive capacity—stimulating domestic demand by expanding the money supply and by increasing government expenditures on goods and services. No significant international consequences were consciously intended.

Remember also that the decisive institution in the process of domestic reflation is the Federal Reserve, which has supplied additional cash balances to the domestic financial markets through the open market purchases of government securities described above. What is likely to be the economic outcome? The additional supply of money disturbs the previously prevailing equilibrium in the market for cash balances. The new excess cash balances are now used by some profit-maximizing holders to purchase so-called income-producing cash equivalents. (Initially most of them purchase pure interest risk financial claims, e.g., government securities.) The increased demand for government securities, all other things being equal, raises the price of government securities and simultaneously lowers the interest rate they bear. Thus, money market interest rates tend to decline so long as the original disturbance—the excess supply of cash balances created by the Federal Reserve—prevails in the money market. As the Federal Reserve continues its policies of directly or indirectly financing the Federal fiscal deficit by buying government debt securities, it continues to supply short-run excess cash balances to the money market, thus maintaining the downward pressure on short-term interest rates.

If this were the end of the financial market process, we might begin to anticipate the expansionist effects the policy makers desired. But because national fiscal and monetary policies are carried out in a relatively open and integrated world economy (and what is more today, in a world of floating exchange rates), declining interest rates on the United States money market will lead United States arbitragists, dealers, and speculators in government securities, who might have sold government securities for cash to the Federal Reserve system, to shift some excess dollar cash balances abroad in search of higher short-term foreign interest rates. Sales (in the foreign-exchange market) of excess dollar cash balances for foreign currencies, all other things being equal, will bring about a decline in the value of the dollar against foreign currencies. And if the sale of dollars against foreign currencies goes on, in response to the continuing drop in relative United States interest rates, brought about in this case by the Federal Reserve's open market operations, the value of the dollar must continue to decline. The excess supply of dollars in the market can only be absorbed at ever lower prices, which is to say, at a continually falling dollar-exchange rate. The decline of the dollar will be arrested only when the demand for dollar cash balances increases to the point where the demand for dollars equals the rising supply, as, for example, it must when the general price level in dollars rises, or when the volume of economic activity increases, or when the Federal Reserve, the source of excess dollar supplies, ceases its open market operations.

Inflation begins, that is to say, the general price level will rise, when the excess supply of dollar cash balances ceases merely to be exported for the purposes of interest rate arbitrage and is used in addition to purchase goods and services domestically. If the foreign-exchange value of the dollar declines more rapidly than the national price level rises, the relative price of our dollar manufactured exports, all other things being equal, will decline below the price of the same goods of foreign competitors, priced and invoiced in the rising foreign currencies. As a result, American export industries will be stimulated; similar foreign export industries will contract. Moreover, as the dollar declines in value abroad, the United States economy may become relatively more attractive to foreign long-term direct investment. Since the dollar prices of some foreign manufactured imports will have risen in the short run, the production of lower-priced substitutes made in the United Staetes will be encouraged, especially if there are substantial unemployed domestic manufacturing resources available. Unemployment in the affected foreign industries could develop quickly. If the affected foreign industries and labor unions have powerful lobbies, foreign governments, hoping to protect domestic employment levels, might become concerned enough to think about trade and exchange controls, or competitive currency depreciation.

Thus, the understandable and perhaps innocent initiative by the United States to raise its own domestic employment levels by means of expansionist domestic monetary policies can give rise to an international economic struggle over appropriate currency exchange rates and export-import policies. It goes without saying that similar reflationary economic policies in, say, France or Germany (if as a result of which their money supply growth rates were to exceed that of the United States) would very likely occasion a depreciation of the French franc and the German mark against the dollar, leading under similar circumstances to precisely the same international economic consequences. The point of this extended analysis is straightforward: There is, in an open world economy, a tragic irony inherent in expansionist government demand management policies. National policy makers, intent exclusively and quite understandably on solving domestic unemployment problems, unconsciously cause disturbances in international financial markets by virtue of expanding fiscal deficits and the creation of excess money supplies. The inevitable international results (for example, the unintended depreciation of the dollar) are subsequently interpreted by foreign governments as diabolical and narrowly nationalistic efforts to export unemployment and to expand domestic economic activity at the expense of one's neighbors. National policy makers will and do argue that they have no conscious exchange-rate policy in mind. They will protest that they merely let the market decide the appropriate exchange-rate relationships. They appear to be genuinely unaware of the relationship of expansionist domestic money-supply policies to foreign exchange-rate changes even as they describe the monetary links to domestic price inflation. As we have observed, these exchange-rate changes are brought about unwittingly by the sometimes obscure mechanism of international arbitrage. We know that a country's reflationary policies may not be intentionally joined to a policy of exchange-rate depreciation; but to a foreign government, which may care only about the shrinking market for some of its overpriced manufactured exports and the related rising unemployment, it makes little difference.

The unforeseen international consequences of expansionist domestic economic policies, engineered purely to reduce national unemployment, are felt quite promptly in a world system of flexible exchange rates. Volatile exchange-rate changes, during a time of high international unemployment, could pit nation against nation in a setting of mutual recrimination and "beggar-my-neighbor" policies. National policy makers, however, rarely realize that international arbitrage transmits most economic disturbances from one nation to another. Most importantly, they seem to ignore the fact that economic disturbances, which are created by fiscal and monetary policies within a dominant economy (especially in a system of floating exchange rates), are rapidly arbitraged throughout the world, often with destructive and destabilizing effects. Is it, then, too much to say to these government policy makers that, in order to ensure global price stability, national policies must be as consistent with the requirements of international economic order as they are with the national interest of domestic full employment?

We now know that if hyperactive national full-employment policies lead to inflationary excess, this inflationary instability must be transmitted to the international system as well. As a result, hoped-for domestic-employment benefits might easily be outweighed by the very real consequences of international economic disturbances. Accordingly, is it unreasonable to suggest that in order to end national monetary disorder and therewith to stabilize the general price level, one genuine alternative open to government policy makers might be to subscribe to the impartial rules of an efficient and enforceable international monetary system, the very operating principle of which might forestall inflationary national monetary and fiscal policies? If it is true, as some argue today, that inflationary economic policies are imposed upon reluctant political authorities by powerful sectarian lobbies, one convenient discipline, available to these same authorities, would be a constitutionally binding monetary treaty which might have the effect of stiffening governmental resistance to these special interest lobbies. Political authorities who ought anyway to say NO to sectarian demands for excessive monetary and fiscal policies (because such policies are unreasonable, unfair, and disruptive of international stability) would certainly be strengthened if their veto were backed by a duly established *constitutional* rule—an international exchange-rate treaty. This line of reasoning leads us directly into the present international debate over the relative merits of fixed- and float-ing-exchange rates.

Fixed or Floating Exchange Rates

Currently it is fashionable to believe that floating-exchange rates can effectively uncouple a national monetary system from the world system. Floating, it has been argued, can pre-vent the transmission of inflation from one country to another.

Monetarists as well as neo-Keynesians have argued that benign neglect of currency exchange rates would yield the benefits of a truly national monetary policy and provide, if desired, a defense against imported inflation. Interestingly, this view has coincided with the recent rise of economic na-tionalism throughout the world. Moreover, a policy of benign neglect in the United States would, some have said, release the Federal Reserve Board from the constraints of the postwar fixed-exchange-rate regime and dollar convertibility. In addi-tion, it was argued, such a policy would allow United States authorities to carry out the necessary national policies to achieve the goal of domestic full employment. These argu-ments against the Bretton Woods regime have become the conventional wisdom of the postwar period. During the past few years, they have formed the basis of the international monetary policy of the United States government. During this period the nation has experienced the suspension of dollar convertibility, two price freezes, price control Phases I, II, III, and IV (between 1971 and 1974), two attempts at setting "stable but adjustable" exchange-rate parities, a super boom, and endemic inflation. The subsequent precipitous decline in commodity prices and national output, combined with a 8-9 percent domestic unemployment, not to mention similar phenomena worldwide, suggest that floating-exchange rates are not the panacea for our domestic and international economic problems. Advocates of floating exchange rates argue that the present exchange-rate system (or the lack thereof) has had insufficient *time* to do its stabilizing handiwork. The point is, of course, that economic policy making and monetary management is not merely a question of technique. Economic policy making is essentially political and normative in its nature. It has to do with the appropriate limits to be placed on individual action in civil society and the appropriate limits to be imposed upon national power in an integrated world economic system; that is, generally speaking, we should determine to what extent national interests should override individual interests or global interests override national. In practice, however, we must not only find the proper limits, but we must also organize the most efficient institutional arrangements to determine and to guard those limits. The chief institutional issue, as it affects the world financial system, may be simply stated: Since we know that the desired balance in world economic relations cannot be sustained without *required* government self-restraint, is there any reason to believe that national self-discipline will endure without an established international monetary system, the efficacious regulating mechanism of which might tend to enforce the needed domestic discipline? It is true that no international monetary reform, in the absence of minimum good will among nations, can be relied upon to underwrite balance and order in the world economy. Undisciplined great powers can destroy any system. But agreed-upon simple rules, rooted in enlightened understanding of national self-interest, and solemnized by treaty organizations, can obviously help to mobilize the forces for domestic self-restraint.

At the moment, fixed-rate systems are unfashionable in many circles. We have, after all, experienced a fixed-rate regime throughout a good part of the postwar era—the much criticized Bretton Woods system. It collapsed in 1971, if not indeed before. But the Bretton Woods international monetary system *was* a *defective* fixed-exchange rate regime, not because, as the advocates of floating would have it, *all* fixed-rate regimes must fail, but because Bretton Woods lacked the essential and impartial rule of universal currency convertibility into gold. The Bretton Woods system was doomed to extinction as a simple consequence of the privilege and the burden it imposed upon the reserve currency status of the dollar which, among other things, led to the dollar's overvaluation and to regularly recurring United States balance-of-payments deficits. The overvaluation of the dollar was the mirror image of the undervalued national currencies of our export competitors, whose manufactures invaded the United States domestic market and displaced certain United States manufactured goods abroad.

Inevitably, the Bretton Woods system, undermined as it was by the permanent balance-of-payments deficit of the reserve-currency country, led to spreading inflation and world financial disequilibrium. Foreign nations perceived United States balance-of-payments deficits as dollar imperialism, while the United States perceived the same deficits as one result of the growing burdens of The Bretton Woods agreement, which symbolized American financial and military leadership throughout the postwar world. The desire to be rid of the unshared financial burdens of leadership provoked economic nationalism in the United States, since increasingly strident demands from the United States for burden-sharing were partially rejected by not entirely responsive foreign allies. At the same time, economic nationalism arose in Europe as a way of protecting European economies from the pervasive inflation which resulted from the permanent American balance-of-payments deficits. For, under the reserve-currency system of the Bretton Woods regime, American balance-of-payments deficits were automatically converted into an expansion of other national money supplies through purchases by European and Japanese central banks of the excess dollars in their financial systems.

Is it any wonder that the Bretton Woods system collapsed? Such a defective fixed-exchange-rate regime, based as it was upon the insupportable privileges and onerous burdens of a reserve-currency system, survived longer than past history suggests it should have. The same official reserve-currency system, based on the pound sterling, had been established in the Western world by the Monetary Conference in Genoa in 1922. This earlier form of the reserve-currency system, called the gold-exchange standard, had collapsed nine years later in 1931, during the early stages of the world depression. Even before 1914, the *unofficial* world reserve-currency system, based largely on sterling convertibility, had shown incipient tendencies toward instability, which had culminated, of course, in the collapse of the gold standard and sterling convertibility at the onset of World War I.

The classical liberal perspective provides, in my view, the definitive objection to a national currency serving as the world curency in either a fixed or a floating exchange-rate regime. For it raises the fundamental historical and theoretical issue: Can one truly expect a national currency to perform its function as a store of value and a medium of exchange, over the long run, beyond its territorial borders, simply because in the short run one observes that the optimal reserve-currency area coincides with the prevailing dominant economic order of the moment? Some suggest that as long as nation-states differ in size and wealth, their optimum currency areas must extend far beyond their territorial borders. History, they argue, ordains the development of reserve currencies and with them must come the risks inherent in such an international financial system. This argument certainly derives some support from the history of the gold and gold-exchange standards of the past one hundred years. Both the pound sterling and the United States dollar during the past century emerged as the world's primary reserve currencies, not least because governments and banks throughout the international system often chose voluntarily to use them as the official basis for the creation of national money supplies.

But history supports even more decisively the view that reserve-currency systems eventually break down, with real and often disastrous economic consequences. Almost all economic historians agree that the collapse of sterling in 1931 was closely associated with the duration and severity of one of the longest depressions in modern history. The suspension of dollar convertibility in 1971 terminated the rule of the ailing Bretton Woods fixed-exchange-rate regime; the subsequent fall of the dollar-exchange rate is clearly associated with the intensification of world inflation between 1972 and 1974. The ensuing world economic contraction has not been as severe as that of the 1930s, but the role of the dollar, as the unimpeachable official reserve currency in the Western world, is surely less certain. Foreign national authorities increasingly realize (as they debate the relative merits of SDRs, dollars, and gold) that as long as the world currency has a national monetary identity, its value will be determined largely by the monetary policies of a single dominant country, the self-discipline of which cannot be taken for granted.

In addition, exemption from effective convertibility requirements tempts the country providing the reserve currency to economic and political excess, which may lead to impossibly ambitious social programs at home and imperial projects abroad. Moreover, history suggests that a reserve currency such as the post-World War II dollar tends toward overvaluation, a monetary condition which may subject its national community to the burden of unemployment in certain labor-intensive manufacturing industries. Prolonged unemployment in certain economic sectors, especially those promptly responsive to world competition, has often afflicted those countries when unrealistic exchange rates prevailed for a long while (as with England between 1925 and 1931). Moreover, destabilizing flows of international capital (as well as unemployment in the country that supplies the reserve currency) have resulted when mercantilist national competitors have stablized their currency values against the reserve currency at a level below the equilibrium exchange rate for the two currencies (as for example, France did against sterling in 1928 and once more against the dollar in 1958 and 1959).

The fact is that no fixed-exchange-rate regime, based on *official* reserve currencies, can be any more secure than the prevailing asymmetrical international political relationships which is reflected at its foundation. Thus, as the postwar international political and financial system changed dramatically after the restoration of currency convertibility in 1958 in Europe, so the national participants in the Bretton Woods system changed their estimates of its costs and benefits. Since the consequences of growing financial disequilibrium created tension and imposed hardships both on the system's leader, as well as upon others, economic nationalism gradually developed throughout the Western alliance, and along with it the incidental desire for independent national monetary policies.

While economic nationalism is a symptom of the world disorder from which it develops, it may also be the necessary midwife of a new global equilibrium. Seen from the global standpoint of those who desire a balanced world financial order, the accelerating tendency toward economic nationalism and volatile exchange-rate changes has served to purge the contemporary world of the profound monetary disequilibrium which developed during the rise and fall of the Bretton Woods reserve-currency system. Therein, in my view, lies some part of the economic meaning of the period through which we are now living. And therein, indeed, lies the significance of the current system of floating exchange rates. If, in the absence of the now discredited Bretton Woods fixed-exchange-rate system, governments do not intend to coordinate monetary policies and therefore will not agree to create an efficient and lasting stable exchange-rate regime, then floating exchange rates must prevail, as they are clearly the most effective instruments of contemporary nationalistic monetary policies. Independent and undisciplined national monetary policies are in fact the indispensable tools of resurgent economic insularity.

The development of intensified economic nationalism throughout the great nations of the Western world is, I have tried to argue, the necessary counterpart of the decline of the intrinsically defective Bretton Woods reserve-currency system and of the international financial disorder such a system engendered. But, to repeat an earlier point, the Bretton Woods experience does not discredit the attempt to establish stable exchange rates. A fixed-exchange-rate regime need not be based upon reserve currencies. Indeed, official reserve currencies are neither desirable nor necessary in the international system. In the long run, they serve neither nations nor individuals very well.

In the end, nations and individuals will conduct their financial operations in those currencies which minimize the financial cost of doing business. Men and nations seek stable currency values in which to denominate financial assets. Accordingly, one might argue that if it is within the power of men and nations to determine their financial policies, then it must be within the reach of the same nations to stabilize and thereby to encourage the domestic use of their own currencies. Moreover, if it is within the power of a nation-state to determine its own monetary policy, then it must be equally within its power to exclude foreign-exchange reserve from its *official* monetary base. To exclude foreign-exchange reserves from the official national monetary base would, then and there, terminate the privilege of the reserve-currency country to run permanent balance-of-payments deficits. Terminating the historic privilege to run permanent balance-of-payments deficits by the reserve-currency country would remove the central defect of the postwar Bretton Woods system. Balance-of-payments deficits in the reserve-currency country would no longer result in an excessive growth of the domestic money supply in those nations whose central banks were required to purchase the excess foreign exchange resulting from the reserve-currency deficit. The domestic inflation, arising in those creditor nations which monetize the deficits of the reserve-currency country, would cease. The tendency toward overvaluation of the former reserve currency would be arrested, and the temptation for mercantilist national competitors to capitalize the presumed export advantages of their undervalued currencies would cease too.

One might go on to argue that in an impartial fixed-exchange-rate regime based upon the efficient regulating mechanism of gold convertibility, synchronization of national monetary growth rates would not need some utopian degree of policy coordination by national authorities. Rather, the very operating principle of such a system—unlimited gold convertibility of external currency liabilities of all banks of issue—would bring about, by an invisible hand, if I may be pardoned the expression, just that coordination of monetary growth rates which rival sovereign states find almost impossible to achieve at conferences and through deliberate international planning. Monetary policy coordination should, of course, be a principal advantage of an efficient fixed-rate system.

In a floating system, or in a fixed-rate regime based on reserve currencies, no such impartial and efficient mechanism exists for the purpose of insuring coordination of national monetary policies. Moreover, coordination or cooperation are words empty of meaning in a flexible exchange-rate system, because different national policy makers have different domestic goals which they will pursue vigorously with conflicting monetary and fiscal policies. On the other hand, a stable international exchange-rate regime with convertibility, supplemented by the money supply elasticities of a sophisticated central- and commercial-banking system, insures both liquidity and the harmonization of different national economic goals in a noninflationary world financial system, by reason of the very nature of the international regulating mechanism.

Why is the rule of gold convertibility an impartial and

efficacious regulating mechanism? The simple rule of monetary convertibility imposes limitations on the quantity of external financial claims created by all banks of issue, and, as a result, requires of them a prudent sense of proportion with respect to the growth of their fiduciary issue, that is, the convertible currency. Moreover, to require the central bank, or any bank of issue, to guarantee unlimited currency convertibility into gold of a fixed weight deters any inflationary increase in the money supply with the threat of bankruptcy. When a commercial bank cannot meet the monetary claims for conversion into gold by its creditors, the end result is liquidation and extinction. For any central bank which creates excess supplies of money the failure to satisfy international claims for conversion results in the suspension of gold payments and subsequent national currency depreciation. The discipline of bankruptcy in a free and open market is the unavoidable penalty of financial excess. The obligation to maintain currency convertibility at fixed rates *limits* the near-monopoly power of government monetary authorities to create excessive money supplies, thereby closing the floodgates to potential inflationary financial tides. Furthermore, the convertibility rule institutionalizes among the great trading nations the public good of a neutral international money, and tends to perpetuate the world economic benefits of global price stability. Reasonable men know that just as civilized liberties cannot endure without individual self-restraint and social discipline, free markets cannot operate efficiently without monetary order. Monetary convertibility embodies the classical principle of order and proportion in a financial system.

Money and Monopoly

Convertibility is more than just a classical principle; in fact, it serves the public interest, for money is a public good. In modern times, the creation of money has almost always been the near-monopoly privilege of the state. State monopoly, like all others, needs regulation. A convertible fixed-exchange-rate regime represents an application to monetary theory of the principle of public-interest monopoly regulation in an imperfectly competitive free market. Allow me to develop this point at length.

For a start, the reasons for considering money a public good are obvious. Money, for example, is a store of value for the nation at large. All American citizens depend on money and near-money equivalents as long-term stores of value for their savings and pensions. Working people expect the purchasing power of their saved earnings to retain, over the long run, the value accorded their labor at the time they chose to forego current consumption at prices then prevailing. In short, the public at large depends on an equitable political community to ensure the value of its monetary savings, which have been, in good faith, laid up in financial assets for future contingencies. Furthermore, in an economy where generalized barter is not a prevailing alternative, money is the universal means of payment and the informational means by which goods are indexed, priced, and publicized. Entrepreneurs will not happily accept money payment for goods, and free working people will not confidently offer their labor in the market, if payment is tendered in an uncertain token, the real purchasing power of which is depreciating. A universally acceptable, stable, unit of account is therefore primarily a public good. Published money prices, because of their mathematical simplicity, are easily accessible forms of public information whereby people are enabled to make intelligent choices between easily calculated alternatives. Generally available, standardized numerical information on prevailing prices in the market is a public good.

Money units of account are the means by which contracts stipulate the purchasing value of deferred payments. If the money unit of account does not retain its value, the community as a whole will cease to make long-term contracts either to invest or to receive money payments in the future. (The limited protection of forward markets provides an esoteric form of security unavailable and unknown to the general public.) Universal willingness to contract in money terms for investment purposes is a national good because national savings are the essential and reliable sources of domestic investments. Savings are the means by which entrepreneurs and innovators find financing for desirable social and economic investments. Investment is the wellspring from which the flow of new and more productive jobs proceeds. The public good of long-run full employment is therefore directly related to the enduring value of money payments. It is this great significance of money as a public good, similar some say to national defense, which has justified placing its regulation in the hands of a state monopoly. In the United States, the Constitution expressly reserved to Congress the monopoly power to regulate coin and currency. In the past, Congress has shared and delegated this power to the commercial banking system. In 1913, Congress delegated to the Federal Reserve, the United States central bank, a near regulatory monopoly over the national money supply.

In an essentially free-market system, government monopoly, like any other, must be controlled. Why? In order to maintain an efficient free market over the long run, a society must rule out or regulate excessively concentrated economic power; otherwise, such power tends to eliminate that competition and free-market entry which are the defining characteristics and principal justifications for a private enterprise economy. Accordingly, if it is decided, for whatever reason, to charter a monopoly within a free-market system, that monopoly should be disciplined in order to forestall the abuse of a power not otherwise regulated by competitive open-market alternatives.[12]

There are, generally speaking, two efficient ways to regulate a monopoly in a competitive open-market economy. The community must either regulate the price of the monopoly's product or service, while making a limited supply impartially available to the free market; or the community must regulate the supply while making the product impartially available and letting open-market demand set the price. In short, in most cases, a free and open market system is the most efficient economic regulator; in the special case where monopoly conditions prevail, a regulated (fixed) price or a regulated (fixed) quantity is the only efficient and equitable rule. Constrained as it is by a regulated price or a regulated quantity for the supply of its product, the monopoly cannot levy an unconscionable price, nor can it improperly withhold or overexpand the supply of its product in an otherwise open market.

From time immemorial, the regulation of money has been held to be a public good, and has often been, therefore, a monopoly privilege of the sovereign political power. How does this particular form of monopoly fit into our general theory? In historical circumstances where the supply of money was primarily a monopoly of government, four basic conditions developed in the market: (1) The government supplied money to the market as it pleased, in whatever quantity it chose, to satisfy whatever result it ordained. Arbitrary abuse of this monopoly privilege led to monetary disorders and therefore to a public desire to discipline money creation. Thus, (2) the government regulated (or fixed) the quantity of money supplied to the market and (often through the supplementary means of interest-rate variations) permitted participants in a free market to compete on an equal footing for the available cash balances. Or (3) the government fixed the universally effective price of its money for both domestic and international purposes. The price of such "real," or so-called commodity, money was often fixed by weight in gold or silver. For example, the price of a "real" money might be made equal to an established weight unit of gold: so many units of money for so many ounces of the real commodity. The price of a "nominal" money (nominal in that the price of the money token, say paper, was not fixed in relation to a real commodity) was often fixed in terms of a unit of foreign currencies. In both nominal and real cases, national or community money had a fixed price, and in order to maintain the fixed price, governments were constrained to conform the supply of money to the demand for it; otherwise, a paucity or an excess would in the long run, cause the price of money (its exchange rate or gold value) to vary substantially from the regulated price. Substantial variation in the price of money caused intense inflation or deflation. Economic disorder engendered social conflict between the beneficiaries and the disinherited of rapidly changing money values. An equitable and cohesive society therefore learned to stabilize the value (that is, the price and quantity) of money in order to avoid social disorder and class war. Or, finally (4), often as a result of confusion, vacillating governments have mixed up two or three available techniques for regulating money in order to manipulate the supply of money to serve changing and special economic purposes.

Today, the same basic alternatives remain. Before proceeding further, we might recall how governments actually intervene to control the money supply in the market. In a free market, the central bank cannot, in fact directly *control* the demand for money. The demand for cash balances arises from the needs and preferences of the market participants, only one of which is the government. The central bank has only a regulatory monopoly over the supply of currency and commercial bank reserves, as it is the banker of last resort. Monetary policy may therefore *influence* the demand for money, but the total demand for real cash balances is determined largely by the preferences of the money users in the market. These users vary their cash balances in response to many influences—e.g., income levels, price levels, interest rates, and expectations about the future real value of money. As long as the supply of money does not exceed the demand for it in the market, money will retain a stable purchasing value. If the government or the central bank sustains, over the long run, an undesired expansion of the nominal supply of money for whatever purpose, without offering a commensurate real value in the market, the purchasing value of money will of course depreciate and the general price level will rise. An excess supply of money, like an excess supply of any commodity, becomes a "drug" in the market, causing thereby a decline in its value and a rise in the nominal value of all goods and services. This monetary process is, of course, the familiar process of inflation: It originates in the abuse of government monopoly power over money; and along with monetary depreciation goes the depreciation of the public trust in government.

I have argued that in a generally free economy (and in the absence of a free and open market in the supply and demand for money), two potentially efficient ways exist for society to limit the government's regulatory monopoly over the supply of cash: fixing supply (the quantity) or fixing price (the exchange rate or gold value). In the first method, the community can regulate (fix), through institutional means, the quantity of money (cash balances) available in the market, such that the supply of money expands only to meet the necessary demands of the free market. Since, in a free society, cash balances must be earned or borrowed in the market, those who demand them, or any other product or service, must offer to the market a commensurate real supply of their labor, their goods, or credit-worthy securities. Thus the market for cash balances and the general price level, in an economy free of government intervention, tend toward equilibrium. There is no way to obtain additional cash balances (nor to demand goods if one holds steady his existing cash balances) without offering to the market an offsetting supply. The inability to demand from society without offering a supply fundamentally alters human behavior. Men will produce for the market in order to consume. Such a stable market process, and the society characterized by it, must tend toward general equilibrium. Moreover, since in a properly regulated monetary system an equilibrium supply of cash balances will never be permitted to exceed for long the demands for them in the market, the value of money too would remain stable. (The *price* of money is in this sense the *reciprocal* of the general price level. Both would be stable and enduring values; that is, they would tend toward unity, as long as general equilibrium prevails.)

In the second method, where government stabilizes the money supply, the nation fixes its currency-exchange rate, that is, for example, the price of its money in exchange for the money of other nations. We remember that supply and demand for a monopoly service must, *generally speaking*, be precisely balanced in order to maintain a regulated price. If the exchange rates of national monies, that is, their prices, are fixed, then governments, or central and commercial banks, may supply money in response to the demands of the market only in quantities which do not disturb that precise balance between the supply and demand for cash balances which is required to maintain, *in this particular case*, the fixed-exchange prices of different national monies. In other words, the central bank's monopoly power to regulate monetary reserves is limited by the requirement to maintain a fixed exchange rate in an open world economy, a rate which becomes impossible to maintain when the long-run supply of national currency balances in the foreign-exchange market exceeds the demand for them. Thus, by fixing the price of currencies, national communities create a discipline which limits the monopoly power of the central bank to supply monetary reserves and currency to the commercial banking system.

This analysis of the means by which to control the government monopoly over money is, of course, appropriate in a floating as well as in a fixed international exchange-rate system. But maintaining stable national money values in a floating exchange-rate system by voluntarily limiting the quantity of cash balances invariably becomes a government policy subject to the usual domestic political pressures. It is a policy deprived of that support which comes in the fixed-rate system from a solemn treaty obligation. Some laissez-faire monetarists, particularly some advocates of floating exchange rates, argue that the value of money should be determined just like other prices, such as those for cotton and copper. Their argument, of course, naively overlooks the monopoly conditions which influence the supply and demand for money in the world market. For if the market for the supply of national currencies lacks the essential regulating mechanism of free entry and open competition, uninfluenced by government power, then some other discipline must be created to contain the autonomy of national-currency systems.

Moreover, floating-exchange-rate proponents make arguments similar to those made by anarchists who assert that written constitutions, the rule of law, the courts, and the police are all gratuitous institutions, having very little social utility because, in their absence, social order ultimately emerges anyway through ruthless and unrestrained competition in the street. We know, however, that the rule of law, far from being inconsistent with an open and free society, is its preliminary condition. Likewise, fixed exchange rates are not only consistent with the principle of the market economy; they are absolutely essential in a free and open world economy where governments monopolize the responsibility of assuring the public good by regulating the supply of money. The contractual rules of a regime of fixed exchange rates are similar in effect to the rule of law among competing individuals (newly arrived, we may imagine, from the jungle) who hope to organize themselves into a free but ordered society.

Toward a Neoclassical System of Contained National Currencies

It has been said recently that if central bankers already understand the need for self-imposed restraint in the interests of the world economic system as a whole, then what logical purpose does it serve to elaborate the rule governing the fixed exchange-rate regime which requires them to do so? If, on the other hand, they lack the understanding or power, they cannot act to uphold any exchange-rate system, including a fixed one.

Such an argument overlooks the fact that in the real world there is a very great difference between a self-imposed deferral of a short-term benefit and the legal requirement to do so. A legal requirement establishes only one barrier between national policy making and narrow national self-interest, but it is often a formidable one. Though reasonable men and lawyers may fully understand a general appeal to equity, defined and strict rules of procedure nevertheless govern their behavior in court. So it is with the simple rule of currency convertibility in a global fixed exchange-rate regime. The rule articulates and establishes a simple basis for international economic order. When nations agree to abide by an inherently efficient international monetary rule, coordinated and disciplined national monetary policies must be the incidental results. Such results are the anti-inflationary foundation for world economic stability. Of course, the rules of a regime based on fixed exchange rates are no more effective than the will and power of the great nations to maintain them. But a minimum rule is more effective than none at all, as minimal social order is preferable to total anarchy. There exists, of course, no international economic or political order which sovereign nations cannot undo. Only precautionary measures, such as exchange-rate treaties, are left to us. Exchange-rate treaties serve to symbolize and to give contractual effect to the acknowledged intent of several great nations, at certain moments in their history, to uphold world economic stability by harmonizing national price levels through coordinated noninflationary money supply growth rates.

Fixed exchange-rate regimes usually originate during historical periods in which men and nations recognize the useful limits on sovereign national power, and then agree contractually to restrain national policy making in the interest of a balanced international order. However, as I have argued, floating rates have often been relied upon during periods of war or resurgent economic nationalism, and they have frequently led to competitive monetary depreciations and neomercantilist national policies.

At Bretton Woods in 1944 the United States initiated and accepted the rule of fixed rates and dollar convertibility in order to insure international price stability in an open world trading system and to facilitate coordinated national economic policies. But the Bretton Woods monetary system, as we have seen, developed the basic defect of national reserve currencies. As the drama of the troubled dollar, the central reserve currency, played itself out during the balance-of-payments crises of the 1960s, not only did other nations begin to resist the Bretton Woods system, but the United States itself finally dealt it the final blow in August of 1971.

The gradual coming of flexible exchange-rate policies in the early 1970s symbolized America's renunciation of its former position as world economic stabilizer. After President Nixon's formal suspension of dollar convertibility into gold, on August 15, 1971, many nations naturally ceased to identify the depreciating dollar with the public good of world financial order which the convertible dollar had underwritten after World War II. International debate continues over the more narrowly conceived domestic and foreign economic policies which have supplanted those which were encouraged by the Bretton Woods system. From the United States point of view, dollar depreciation was brought about by the market as a result of uncoordinated national policies. From the viewpoint of others, dollar depreciation was brought about by a United States monetary policy designed primarily to limit merchandise imports and encourage domestically manufactured substitutes, to curtail long-term United States investment abroad, to encourage exports of goods and short-term United States capital, and to stimulate long-term capital imports into the United States. These objectives, some argue, would be con-

sistent with the goal of domestic full employment in an expanding and profitable national economy.[13] Such a distinction
of viewpoints will make little difference to some trading
partners of the United States because they will, in any event,
be confronted with the loss of traditional markets for their
goods. In retaliation, certain nation-states and their trading
partners may develop general protectionist or preferential
trading patterns with so-called natural trading partners, not to
mention competitive exchange-rate policies and tax and credit
subsidies to their export sectors.

Stable monetary values and future global financial equilibrium are unlikely to develop, as some abstractly argue, in the
form of de facto stable exchange rates, which would simulate a
fixed-rate regime. Monetary stabilization will result more
probably as the by-product of a convertible fixed exchange-
rate regime, imposed upon the world (as in the past) by several
leading nations. Whether the world has fixed or floating exchange rates does matter in that it reflects the extent to which
self-seeking great powers intend to be bound by a minimum of
conventions agreed upon by all. Few explicit limitations are
acknowledged by sovereign powers in a floating monetary system. To be sure, the absence of a peace treaty among former
belligerents does not suggest an imminent state of war. Nor
does the absence of a fixed exchange-rate regime necessarily
imply economic warfare. It is difficult to miss, however, the
contrasting implications of the two different sets of conditions. If the great trading nations genuinely do not intend to
seek short-run advantages by adopting "beggar-my-neighbor"
policies, as their finance ministers and central bankers claim at
almost every contemporary international conference, and if
they actually mean to concert their economic and monetary
policies, then why should their representatives at the same
time reject the very exchange-rate treaties which are the concrete and reliable means by which to institutionalize the de-
clared intention to coordinate national policies?

The fatal defect of the Bretton Woods regime, as I have

suggested, lay in the reserve currency role of the dollar. Any sound and enduring fixed exchange-rate regime, which takes its place, must insist upon currency convertibility and, in my view, must rule out the use of a national currency as an *official* world currency. No national currency can form the long-term stable basis upon which other nations can issue their own domestic currencies. As I argued before, the burdens of a world reserve currency must prove intolerable both for the issuing nation and the international system at large. Two hundred nation-states will inevitably disagree about the objectives of monetary policy in the reserve-currency country. However, if the *official* status of the national monetary standard is strictly limited to the banking and currency system of the country of issue, then we shall have met one of the political preconditions for a new global equilibrium. The new international monetary order must *prohibit* central banks from purchasing and holding foreign-exchange reserves (against the creation of domestic money). If no domestic money can be created as a result of central-bank monetization of the balance-of-payments deficits of other countries, no domestic inflation can therefore result from the imbalance in the foreign-exchange market caused by excess creation of foreign money supplies. This prohibition would also forestall completely the development of an official reserve currency with a national identity, though it would not in any way constrain unofficial (private) accumulations of foreign-exchange balances for current payment or speculative purposes.

Such a system of multiple national monetary and banking systems—the classical design of contained national currency areas—constitutes a necessary, if insufficient, condition for creating a new international financial system for the future. For, as I mentioned at the outset, in the absence of a utopian world government and central bank, the world economy will continue to be governed by its national centers. Only an international arrangement which puts these irreducible national political centers within a contractual regime to uphold fixed rates and convertibility, without *official* reserve currencies, suits the real world. Only such an international monetary system can help to rationalize a globe of competing and jealous nations. Only such a monetary order can sustain rather than deter the further development of a durable, interdependent, growing world-trading system.

The history of the sterling and dollar standards during the past half century illustrates the perils inherent in reserve-currency systems under stress. The umbilical cord of a national reserve currency, run halfway round the globe, should no longer have to provide the financial lifeline for economic growth throughout the world. At the very least, the peril to the international monetary system, inherent in the potential collapse of a national reserve currency, should be ruled out of the world economy. It would be an exaggeration to believe that sterling's collapse as a reserve currency in the 1930s was the basic reason for the economic nationalism and the wars of the 1930s and 1940s, but it would be obtuse to ignore the recurring destructive consequences to world economic order of a reserve-currency system in disarray.

Even if governments should terminate the legal status and forestall the future development of reserve currencies, other fundamental problems will obviously remain. The political, financial, and technical problems of creating a new, universally acceptable means of international payment will have to be faced. Any new system will have to provide for adequate growth in international liquidities, but without undermining the classical requirements of budgetary discipline and price stability in the major trading nations of the world economic system. There is, finally, the problem of the Eurocurrency market, which, after the creation of an efficient and open international monetary order, may well gravitate back to the national centers whose restrictions it originally sought to evade. Nor can we forget that, whatever the formal international system, undisciplined domestic policies in major countries may still grievously distort price and production relationships throughout the world.

One positive result of our present period of floating exchange rates could easily be that fundamental equilibrium of some national currency values will gradually reassert itself. Ironically, perhaps, the end of the official reserve-currency status of the dollar may coincide with an unparalleled resurgency of the more competitive American economy. Economic resurgence, if reenforced by an enduring monetary stabilization in the United States, a stable world price level, and a noninflationary international financial system, must restore the power and the prestige of the world's most efficient economy and the world's most productive people.

Seen in historical perspective, the present world economic disorder, which has been exacerbated by the transitional system of floating exchange rates, must give way in due course to the desire for a system of fixed exchange rates: and this because, in today's floating system, the former reserve currency's volatile exchange rates will bear the burden of frequent adjustment required by everchanging domestic economic policies. These exchange-rate adjustments will be prompt; their real economic consequences will be equally prompt and severe. National (and foreign) political constituencies will not passively endure forever the painful domestic price and production adjustments induced by excessively fluctuating foreign-exchange-rate relationships. These constituencies will coalesce behind the idea of stable exchange rates and non-interventionist government economic policies. I believe that political leadership in the United States will arise to represent these constituencies, as American politicians gradually perceive that no international monetary stabilization will endure without the participation of the world's dominant economy.

In conclusion, I should like to affirm one fundamental article of faith which underlies my view of the limited utility of a national currency. In the interest of international equilibrium and fair play, the currency system of a great power must always be excluded from the more general international role which it has often been called upon to perform. The stability of the global monetary system must be characterized by an absence of national currencies playing the *legally established* international role of world money, though these national currencies may continue to be held at risk, without limit, for whatever purpose, in the cash balances of individuals and corporations throughout the world. Reserve currencies will merely cease to serve as the legal basis for creating money in foreign countries, since reserve currencies will be ruled out of the official monetary base of foreign banking systems.

Because national authorities will be subjected, in an open and floating exchange-rate system, to the immediate inflationary consequences of their domestic economic policy decisions, they may in the end be required by the growing political pressures of their national constituencies, to choose those policies which tend to insure long-run domestic price stability. These policies will include national budgetary discipline and the pursuit of exchange-rate stability. The growing desire for general price stability within major countries will be the essential inspiration of an enduring international monetary system of the future, firmly founded, as I believe it will be, upon a regime of fixed exchange rates based upon convertibility. Surely these financial conditions, and perhaps only these conditions, will make possible the achievement in our time of the national and international goals of long-term full employment, a stable general price level, and low long-term interest rates. The creation of such a world monetary system, under United States leadership, will, I believe, coincide with the end of inflation in the Western world.

Notes

[1] J.M. Keynes, *The General Theory*, Royal Economic Society edition (1973), p. 381.

[2] See the Senate Banking and House Banking Committee Resolutions and Debates of March 1975 on the subject. These resolutions were reported in detail in the daily press.

[3] Robert Mundell, *Monetary Theory* (1971), p. 2.

[4] Immanuel Wallerstein, *The Modern World System*, Volume I: *Capitalist Agriculture and the Origins of the European World-Economy in the Sixteenth Century* (1974), pp. 15-16.

[5] See the section on the definition and function of arbitrage, "The Market Mechanism: Arbitrage," below.

[6] Mundell, *op.cit.*, pp. 1-2.

[7] Another variant of this school of thought is known to its (economic) advocates as the "price and incomes" policy for present day mixed economies. The burden of its method is primarily the substitution of state administered wages and prices for the agency of a more or less free and open market. It has never been entirely clear to me why, in this school of thought, economic liberty receives such cavalier treatment while, for example, the liberty to publish is held in ever higher regard. "Cuius regio cuius religio." In a free society there must be an indissoluble relationship between civil liberties and economic liberty. Contemporary intellectuals separate them in their theories, as no free society can do for long in reality.

[8] On the gold-exchange standard, see the essay of Edmund Lebée, *Les Doctrines Monétaires* (1932). Regarding the historiography of the gold-exchange standard, see the description of and sources on central bank diplomacy in Charles P. Kindleberger, *The World in Depression* (1973), and Alexander de Cecco, *Money and Empire: The International Gold Standard, 1890-1914* (1975). See also the six essays in the Lehrman Institute's forthcoming volume, *Balance of Power or Hegemony: The Interwar Monetary System* (New York University Press, 1976). This collection provides a good bibliography on the continuing scholarly debate concerning the nature and theory of the historic gold and gold-exchange standards. On the problems of the gold-exchange standard in the postwar Bretton Woods era, see, among others, the often antithetical writings of Robert Triffin and Jacques Rueff.

[9] For the discussion of the economics of public goods, I am indebted to C. P. Kindleberger who lent me his (unpublished) essay, "Power in the International Economy: Exploitation, Public Goods, or Free Rides."

[10] See Arthur B. Laffer, "The Phenomenon of Worldwide Inflation: A Study in International Market Integration," in David I. Meiselman and Arthur B. Laffer, eds., *The Phenomenon of Worldwide Inflation* (1975), who cites Moon Hoe Lee's "Excess

Inflation and Currency Depreciation," unpublished Ph.D. dissertation, U. of Chicago Graduate School of Business, 1974. (Lee's data includes, among many other indexes, detailed graphs showing coincident movements of wholesale prices in the United States, the United Kingdom, Canada, France, Germany, Italy, Japan, the Netherlands, and Switzerland between 1900 and 1972.)

[11] Even the Soviet and Chinese economic systems increasingly have been integrated into the international system of world market exchange, where prices are arbitraged across national boundaries. Much of the pertinent data may be unavailable, but it is not implausible to argue that domestic price levels in China and the Soviet Union are increasingly influenced by world market prices. One might study, for example, Soviet COMECON internal pricing techniques in the 1970-1975 Five Year Plan, where traded goods are priced at the level of certain average world prices. These techniques have led to considerable controversy within COMECON because of the dramatic changes in the current world price levels for primary commodities. There is, in addition, the rapidly growing exchange among the nations in the Soviet system, China, and the West. To cite one example:

> Moscow, April 2 (UPI) 1975 - Soviet trade with the West leaped 50 percent last year and now accounts for about one-third of all Soviet foreign trade, the Tass news agency reported today. "This is regarded in official circles as an indication of a new state in the Soviet Union's commercial and economic cooperation with the Western countries," Tass said. The agency did not give figures for trade with the United States but said Western Europe accounted for three-quarters of the Soviet trade turnover with all industrial capitalist countries. "It goes without saying that the Soviet foreign trade figures in dealings with Western countries were affected by increased *world market prices,*" Tass said.

Among the many sources for COMECON pricing techniques, see Edwin Dale's article of April 2, 1975, in *The New York Times,* reporting the Soviet trade surplus with the West, and vis-à-vis the COMECON countries.

[12] Competition among many independent participants in a free and open economy is the essential regulating mechanism of the

public interest. The public has an interest in the lowest possible price. From the standpoint of the consumer, competition tends to reduce flexible prices to the absolute minimum level generally determined by the market expectation of the most efficient and innovative producer. In the absence of the public good of an open economy and free competition, the consumer and producer give up unrestricted access to the market. As a result monopoly conditions develop. Monopoly conditions tend to raise the prices of essential goods and services to the public. If moreover the state *charters* monopoly power over an essential service, the national community *must* forfeit the potential economic benefits which might otherwise be obtained from free market competition to provide the same service. Now, if to uphold the public interest in low prices, there must be equal access to all for the right to supply and demand an essential service, the free and open market, under monopoly conditions, is not available to provide it. Accordingly, if a free society chooses, *for whatever reason*, to charter a monopoly power, society must regulate that power in order to forestall the abuse of privilege which must tempt any sovereign economic authority, unconstrained as it would be by competitive alternatives. The more such regulation simulates the conditions of a free and open market, the more the public interest will surely prevail.

¹³ "In the long run, retention of the monetary leadership in the U.S. will depend on the quality of U.S. performance, with *erratic* or *antisocial* behavior ultimately forcing Europe into a currency coalition. The greater the departure from acceptable norms, the more likely is the emergence of monetary leadership in Europe." Mundell, op. cit., p. 169.